Learning 30 European Languages Through the Lord's Prayer

by Corey Alan Chuba

VITAE PRESS

EMBARK ON YOUR QUEST

Vitae Press

Vitae Press is a publishing house dedicated to exploring the enduring legacy of Western life, thought, and culture as shaped by the Roman tradition. The name *Vitae*, derived from the Latin word for "life," reflects our mission to publish works that engage with the values, ideas, and heritage of the Western world. From fiction to non-fiction to reprints of timeless works from Christendom and Western Civilization, each book seeks to deepen the understanding of the moral, spiritual, and intellectual foundations that have guided generations and continue to inspire today.

TABLE OF CONTENTS

Language Category IV

FOREWORD

For centuries, the *Pater Noster*—the Lord's Prayer—has been more than a prayer. It has been a foundation of faith, a text of memory, and a bridge between peoples. From the first missionaries who carried Christianity across Europe to scholars and polyglots who sought to understand its many tongues, this prayer has served as a common text through which languages could be preserved, compared, and learned.

One of the greatest examples of this method is found in the life of Cardinal Giuseppe Gasparo Mezzofanti (A.D. 1774–1849), a 19th-century A.D. Italian priest and hyperpolyglot renowned for his mastery of languages. According to his biographer Charles William Russell in *The Life of Cardinal Mezzofanti* (A.D. 1858), Cardinal Mezzofanti often began his study of a new language by asking travelers or pilgrims to recite the Lord's Prayer, the Ten Commandments, or the Apostles' Creed in their native tongue. Because these sacred texts were both familiar and translated in a relatively literal way across languages, they provided him with a linguistic "Rosetta Stone." From this foundation, Cardinal Mezzofanti would piece together the grammar, vocabulary, and rhythm of the language, later refining his speech through conversation. His method reflected a deep truth: most daily speech relies on a small set of vocabulary and basic grammatical structures—and the Lord's Prayer provides many of them.

Learning 30 European Languages Through the Lords Prayer

The European languages in which Cardinal Mezzofanti prayed and conversed reflect centuries of history. Alphabets and grammar have always shaped how people communicate. English, for example, uses the Latin alphabet but retains Germanic grammar at its core. Born from Old English—akin to Old Norse and Old German—modern English was reshaped by the Norman Conquest in A.D. 1066, which brought French vocabulary and Latin influence. Thus, English today is a unique blend of Germanic and Romantic elements.

This process was not unique to England. After the fall of Rome (A.D. 476), the Latin alphabet was adopted by the Germanic tribes who entered former Roman territories. Meanwhile, in Eastern Europe, on orders from the Roman Church, Saints Cyril and Methodius created the Cyrillic alphabet to bring the Christian faith to the Slavic peoples. At the same time, the Greeks preserved their own script and grammar, evolving from ancient to modern Greek. These choices of script and grammar still define Europe's linguistic map today.

Of course, some languages are easier for English speakers to learn than others. A familiar alphabet does not always mean an easy grammar, and conversely, an unfamiliar script may conceal a relatively straightforward grammar. Greek, for instance, looks very different on the page but is simpler in structure than Finnish, Estonian, or Hungarian—languages with the Latin alphabet but extremely complex grammar from their Uralic roots.

For this reason, European languages can be grouped into the following broad categories in their ease of learning for English speakers:

- **Category 1**: Romance and easier Germanic languages (Spanish, Portuguese, French, Italian, Dutch, Norwegian, Swedish, Danish, and Romanian).
- **Category 2**: More complex Germanic languages (German and Icelandic).
- **Category 3**: Slavic, Baltic, Celtic, and Greek languages (Greek, Czech, Slovak, Irish, Polish, Serbian, Bulgarian, Croatian, Bosnian, Slovenian, Macedonian, Belarusian, Ukrainian, Russian, Latvian, and Lithuanian).
- **Category 4**: Uralic languages with non-Indo-European origins and very complex grammar (Finnish, Estonian, and Hungarian).

Here is a full list of the languages that we will be going over in this book, in order of ease, with the type of alphabet and then the type of grammar beside them:

Language (Alphabet – Grammar)
English (Latin – Germanic)
Spanish (Latin – Romantic)
Portuguese (Latin – Romantic)
French (Latin – Romantic)
Italian (Latin – Romantic)
Dutch (Latin – Germanic)
Norwegian (Latin – Germanic)
Swedish (Latin – Germanic)
Danish (Latin – Germanic)
Romanian (Latin – Romantic)
German (Latin – Germanic)
Icelandic (Latin – Germanic)
Greek (Greek – Hellenic)
Czech (Latin – W. Slavic)
Slovak (Latin – W. Slavic)

Irish (Latin – Celtic)
Polish (Latin – W. Slavic)
Serbian (Latin & Cyrillic – S. Slavic)
Bulgarian (Cyrillic – S. Slavic)
Croatian (Latin – S. Slavic)
Bosnian (Latin – S. Slavic)
Slovenian (Latin – S. Slavic)
Macedonian (Cyrillic – S. Slavic)
Belarusian (Cyrillic – E. Slavic)
Ukrainian (Cyrillic – E. Slavic)
Russian (Cyrillic – E. Slavic)
Latvian (Latin – Baltic)
Lithuanian (Latin – Baltic)
Finnish (Latin – Uralic)
Estonian (Latin – Uralic)
Hungarian (Latin – Uralic)

Latin, though now called a "dead language," remains vital because of its permanence. It does not evolve with time, which is why the Catholic Church preserves it in the liturgy: the meaning of Scripture and the writings of the Fathers remains unchanged. In this sense, Latin is not dead but timeless.

This book is arranged to make language learning simple and practical. Each language is given six pages:

Page 1: The Lord's Prayer in full, line by line.

Page 2: The Lord's Prayer, word-for-word translation.

Page 3: The Lord's Prayer, phonetic guide for pronunciation.

Page 4: An introduction to the language's alphabet.

Pages 5-6: The basics of the language's grammar.

My purpose is twofold: first, to awaken interest in the languages of Europe, and second, to help Westerners reconnect with their heritage. For those of European descent, this book provides a way to pray as your ancestors once prayed—in their native tongues, or in the Latin and Greek of the early Church. Even if you do not pursue full fluency, you can at least speak the words of the Lord's Prayer in the language of your forefathers. May this work inspire both the mind and the soul: to study the diversity of European languages, and to rediscover the unity of Christian faith that gave them their first shared prayer.

And now I will leave you with the Lord's Prayer in Latin, which in many ways is the most influential of the European languages:

Pater Noster

Pater noster, qui es in cælis,
sanctificetur nomen tuum.
Adveniat regnum tuum.
Fiat voluntas tua, sicut in cælo et in terra.
Panem nostrum quotidianum da nobis hodie,
et dimitte nobis debita nostra,
sicut et nos dimittimus debitoribus nostris.
Et ne nos inducas in tentationem,
sed libera nos a malo.
Amen.

Corey A. Chuba
Pittsburgh, Pennsylvania
October, A.D. 2025

LEARNING 30 EUROPEAN LANGUAGES THROUGH THE LORD'S PRAYER

Chapter I

Spanish

The Lords Prayer in *Español* (Spanish)

El Padre Nuestro

Padre nuestro, que estás en el cielo,
santificado sea tu Nombre;
venga a nosotros tu reino;
hágase tu voluntad,
en la tierra como en el cielo.
Danos hoy nuestro pan de cada día;
perdona nuestras ofensas,
como también nosotros perdonamos
a los que nos ofenden;
no nos dejes caer en la tentación,
y líbranos del mal.
Amén.

Word-to-Word Translation

El Padre Nuestro (The Our Father)

Padre (Father) **nuestro,** (our,)

que (who) **estás** (are) **en** (in) **el** (the) **cielo,** (heaven,)

santificado (sanctified) **sea** (be) **tu** (your) **Nombre;** (Name;)

venga (come) **a** (to) **nosotros** (us) **tu** (your) **reino;** (kingdom;)

hágase (be done) **tu** (your) **voluntad,** (will,)

en (on) **la** (the) **tierra** (earth) **como** (as) **en** (in) **el** (the) **cielo.** (heaven.)

Danos (Give us) **hoy** (today) **nuestro** (our) **pan** (bread) **de** (of) **cada** (each) **día;** (day;)

perdona (forgive) **nuestras** (our) **ofensas,** (offenses,)

como (as) **también** (also) **nosotros** (we) **perdonamos** (forgive) **a** (to) **los** (those) **que** (who) **nos** (us) **ofenden;** (offend;)

no (not) **nos** (us) **dejes** (let) **caer** (fall) **en** (into) **la** (the) **tentación,** (temptation,)

y (and) **líbranos** (deliver us) **del** (from the) **mal.** (evil.)

Amén. (Amen.)

Phonetic Pronunciation

El Padre Nuestro *(El Pah-dreh Nwehs-troh)*

Padre (Pah-dreh) **nuestro** (nwehs-troh) **que** (keh) **estás** (ehs-tahs) **en** (en) **el** (el) **cielo** (see-eh-loh),

santificado (sahn-tee-fee-kah-doh) **sea** (seh-ah) **tu** (too) **Nombre** (nohm-breh);

venga (behn-gah) **a** (ah) **nosotros** (noh-soh-trohs) **tu** (too) **reino** (ray-noh);

hágase (ah-gah-seh) **tu** (too) **voluntad** (boh-loon-tahd) **en** (en) **la** (lah) **tierra** (tee-eh-rah) **como** (koh-moh) **en** (en) **el** (el) **cielo** (see-eh-loh).

Danos (dah-nohs) **hoy** (oy) **nuestro** (nwehs-troh) **pan** (pahn) **de** (deh) **cada** (kah-dah) **día** (dee-ah);

perdona (pehr-doh-nah) **nuestras** (nwehs-trahs) **ofensas** (oh-fehn-sahs),

como (koh-moh) **también** (tahm-byehn) **nosotros** (noh-soh-trohs) **perdonamos** (pehr-doh-nah-mohs) **a** (ah) **los** (lohs) **que** (keh) **nos** (nohs) **ofenden** (oh-fehn-dehn);

no (noh) **nos** (nohs) **dejes** (deh-hehs) **caer** (kah-ehr) **en** (en) **la** (lah) **tentación** (tehn-tah-syohn),

y (ee) **líbranos** (lee-brah-nohs) **del** (del) **mal** (mahl).

Amén (ah-mehn).

Understanding the Spanish Alphabet

Alphabet
- Spanish uses 27 letters: the standard Latin 26 (A–Z) plus Ñ.
- Alphabet order: … N, Ñ, O …
- The letters **K** and **W** are rare and mainly appear in loanwords (*kilómetro, whisky*).
- Traditional digraphs **CH** and **LL** were once counted as separate letters, but since 2010 are alphabetized as *c+h* and *l+l*.

Letter Sounds Differ from English
- **A** = *ah* (casa = kah-sah).
- **E** = *eh* (mesa = meh-sah).
- **I** = *ee* (vino = vee-no).
- **O** = *oh* (sol = sohl).
- **U** = *oo* (luna = loo-nah). Silent after *g/q* unless marked with ¨ (vergüenza = ver-gwen-za).
- **Ñ** = *ny* as in *canyon* (señor = seh-nyor).
- **C before e, i** = *s* (Spain) or *th* (Castilian Spain) → *cena* = seh-nah / theh-nah.
- **C before a, o, u** = hard *k* (casa = kah-sah).
- **Z** = *s* (Latin America) or *th* (Spain) (zapato = sah-pah-to / thah-pah-to).
- **G before e, i** = throaty *h* (general = heh-ne-ral).
- **G before a, o, u** = hard *g* (gato = gah-to).
- **GU before e, i** = hard *g* (guitarra = gee-tar-ra). If ü is marked, *u* is pronounced (pingüino = peen-gwee-no).
- **J** = throaty *h* (jugar = hoo-gar).
- **LL / Y** = in most regions, both sound like *y* (calle = kah-yeh). In parts of Argentina/Uruguay, they are *zh/sh*.
- **R** = tapped *r* between vowels (pero = peh-ro), strongly trilled at the start of words or doubled (perro = peh-rro).
- **H** = always silent (hola = oh-la).
- **V** = usually pronounced like *b* (vino ≈ bee-no).
- **X** = usually *ks* (taxi), but sometimes *h* (México = Meh-hee-ko).

Accent Marks
- Written accents (´) show **where stress falls** when it doesn't follow normal rules: *café, difícil*.
- Distinguish meaning: *tú* (you) vs. *tu* (your), *sí* (yes) vs. *si* (if).
- Words ending in vowel, *n*, or *s* → stress on 2nd-to-last syllable (*casa*).
- Words ending in other consonants → stress on last syllable (*hotel*).

Understanding Spanish Grammar

Nouns and Gender
- Spanish nouns are either **masculine** (usually ending in **-o**, e.g., *el libro* = the book) or **feminine** (usually ending in **-a**, e.g., *la mesa* = the table).
- Some exceptions exist (*el día, la mano*).
- Plural forms: add **-s** to vowels (*libros*), **-es** to consonants (*papeles*).

Articles
- Definite: *el, la, los, las* = the.
- Indefinite: *un, una, unos, unas* = a, an, some.
- Articles must agree with gender and number.

Adjectives
- Normally follow the noun (*casa blanca* = white house).
- Must agree in **gender and number** with the noun:
    - Masculine singular: *niño alto* (tall boy).
    - Feminine singular: *niña alta* (tall girl).
    - Masculine plural: *niños altos*.
    - Feminine plural: *niñas altas*.

Pronouns
- Subject pronouns (often omitted in speech): *yo, tú, él/ella/usted, nosotros, vosotros, ellos/ellas/ustedes*.
- Direct object pronouns: *me, te, lo/la, nos, os, los/las*.
- Indirect object pronouns: *me, te, le, nos, os, les*.
- Reflexive pronouns: *me, te, se, nos, os, se*.

Verbs
- Three main conjugation groups: **-ar, -er, -ir** (hablar, comer, vivir).
- Conjugations change by person, number, tense, and mood.
- Key moods:
    - **Indicative** (statements, facts).
    - **Subjunctive** (wishes, doubts, hypotheticals).
    - **Imperative** (commands).
- Common tenses:
    - **Present tense:** *yo hablo* (I speak).
    - **Preterite tense:** *yo hablé* (I spoke).
    - **Imperfect tense:** *yo hablaba* (I used to speak).

- o **Future tense:** *yo hablaré* (I will speak).
- o **Conditional tense:** *yo hablaría* (I would speak).
- o Compound forms with **haber**:
  he hablado (I have spoken), *había hablado* (I had spoken).

Word Order
- Standard **SVO** (subject-verb-object): *Juan come pan* (Juan eats bread).
- Subject can be dropped since verb endings show who is acting *como pan* (I eat bread).
- For emphasis, Spanish allows flexible word order.

Questions and Negation
- Questions invert subject and verb: *¿Hablas tú español?* (Do you speak Spanish?).
- Yes/No questions are often just marked by intonation.
- Negation: place **no** before verb (*No hablo inglés* = I don't speak English).

Prepositions
- Always followed by object pronouns in their special forms: *para mí* (for me), *conmigo* (with me), *contigo* (with you).
- Common ones: *a* (to), *de* (of/from), *en* (in), *con* (with), *por* (by/through), *para* (for/purpose).

Special Features
- Use of **ser** vs. **estar** (both = to be):
  - o *ser* for permanent traits (*soy alto* = I am tall).
  - o *estar* for temporary states/locations (*estoy cansado* = I am tired).
- Two verbs for "to know":
  - o *saber* (facts, skills).
  - o *conocer* (people, places).
- Double negatives are allowed and required (*no tengo nada* = I don't have anything).

Chapter II

Portuguese

The Lords Prayer in *Português* (Portuguese)

Oração do Senhor

Pai nosso, que estás nos céus,
santificado seja o teu nome;
venha o teu reino;
seja feita a tua vontade,
assim na terra como no céu.
O pão nosso de cada dia nos dai hoje;
perdoa-nos as nossas dívidas,
assim como nós perdoamos aos nossos devedores;
e não nos deixes cair em tentação,
mas livra-nos do mal.
Amém.

Word-to-Word Translation

Oração do Senhor *(The Our Father)*

Pai (Father) **nosso** (our),

que (who) **estás** (are) **nos** (in the) **céus** (heavens),

santificado (sanctified) **seja** (be) **o** (the) **teu** (your) **nome** (name);

venha (come) **o** (the) **teu** (your) **reino** (kingdom);

seja (be) **feita** (done) **a** (the) **tua** (your) **vontade** (will),

assim (thus) **na** (in the) **terra** (earth) **como** (as) **no** (in the) **céu** (heaven).

O (the) **pão** (bread) **nosso** (our) **de** (of) **cada** (each) **dia** (day) **nos** (to us) **dai** (give) **hoje** (today);

perdoa-nos (forgive us) **as** (the) **nossas** (our) **dívidas** (debts),

assim (as) **como** (as) **nós** (we) **perdoamos** (forgive) **aos** (to the) **nossos** (our) **devedores** (debtors);

e (and) **não** (not) **nos** (us) **deixes** (let) **cair** (fall) **em** (into) **tentação** (temptation),

mas (but) **livra-nos** (deliver us) **do** (from the) **mal** (evil).

Amém (Amen).

Phonetic Pronunciation

Oração do Senhor *(El Pah-dreh Nwehs-troh)*

Pai (pah-ee) **nosso** (no-soo),

que (keh) **estais** (es-tahys) **no** (noo) **céu** (seh-oo),

santificado (san-chee-fee-kah-doo) **seja** (seh-zhah) **o** (oo) **vosso** (voh-soo) **nome** (noh-mee);

venha (ven-yah) **a** (ah) **nós** (noos) **o** (oo) **vosso** (voh-soo) **reino** (ray-noo);

seja (seh-zhah) **feita** (fay-tah) **a** (ah) **vossa** (voh-sah) **vontade** (vohn-tah-jee)

assim (ah-seem) **na** (nah) **terra** (teh-hah) **como** (koh-moo) **no** (noo) **céu** (seh-oo).

O (oo) **pão** (pown) **nosso** (no-soo) **de** (jee) **cada** (kah-dah) **dia** (dee-ah) **nos** (noos) **dai** (dah-ee) **hoje** (oh-zhee);

perdoa-nos (pehr-doh-ah-noos) **as** (ahz) **nossas** (noo-sahs) **dívidas** (dee-vee-dahs),

assim (ah-seem) **como** (koh-moo) **nós** (noos) **perdoamos** (pehr-doh-ah-mos) **aos** (ah-oosh) **nossos** (noo-soos) **devedores** (deh-veh-doh-res);

e (eh) **não** (now) **nos** (noos) **deixes** (day-shees) **cair** (kah-eer) **em** (eng) **tentação** (tehn-tah-sow),

mas (mahs) **livra-nos** (lee-vrah-noos) **do** (doo) **mal** (mahl).

Amém (ah-men).

Understanding the Portuguese Alphabet

Alphabet
- Portuguese uses the standard Latin 26 letters (A–Z).
- The letters **K, W, and Y** appear only in foreign words, names, or loanwords.
- Alphabet order: … X, Y, Z.
- Traditional digraphs like **CH, LH, NH, RR, SS, QU, GU** represent unique sounds, not separate letters.

Letter Sounds Differ from English
- **A** = *ah* (casa = kah-zah).
- **E** = open *eh* or closed *ay* (mesa = meh-zah, vê = vay).
- **I** = *ee* (vinho = vee-nyo).
- **O** = open *aw* or closed *oh* (sol = sohl, avô = ah-voh).
- **U** = *oo* (luz = looz). Silent after **q/g** unless marked (linguiça = ling-wee-sa).
- **Á, É, Í, Ó, Ú** (acute) = stressed vowel, distinguishes meaning (*pó* = powder vs. *po* = I put).
- **Â, Ê, Ô** (circumflex) = stressed closed vowels (*avô* = grandfather, você = you).
- **Ã, Õ** (tilde) = nasalized vowels (*pão* = bread, não = no/not).
- **J** = soft "zh" as in English *measure* (jamais = zhah-maish).
- **H** = always silent (hora = oh-rah).
- **R** = varies by position:
  - Initial or double *rr* = guttural throaty *h* (rato = *h*ah-to).
  - Single *r* between vowels = soft tap (caro = kah-ro).
- **S** = *s* at start, *z* between vowels (*sapo* = sah-po, casa = kah-zah).
- **X** = *ks, s,* or *sh* depending on word (*tórax* = toh-ra-ks, xadrez = shah-drez).
- **Double consonants**: generally rare, except **rr, ss**, which change pronunciation.

Accent Marks
- **Acute (´)** = marks stressed vowels (*á, é, í, ó, ú*).
- **Circumflex (ˆ)** = stressed closed vowels (*â, ê, ô*).
- **Tilde (˜)** = nasalized vowels (*ã, õ*).
- **Diaeresis (¨)** = historically marked separate pronunciation (*linguiça*), but no longer used in modern Brazilian Portuguese.
- Accents also distinguish homonyms and guide pronunciation.

Understanding Portuguese Grammar

Nouns and Gender
- Nouns are either **masculine** (usually ending in **-o**, e.g., *o livro* = the book) or **feminine** (usually ending in **-a**, e.g., *a mesa* = the table).
- Some exceptions (*o dia, a mão*).
- Plural forms:
  - Add **-s** if the word ends in a vowel (*livros*).
  - Add **-es** if ending in consonant (*mulheres*).
  - Irregular changes occur (*cão → cães* = dog → dogs).

Articles
- Definite: *o, a, os, as* = the.
- Indefinite: *um, uma, uns, umas* = a, an, some.
- Must agree with gender and number of the noun.

Adjectives
- Usually follow the noun (*casa bonita* = beautiful house).
- Must agree in gender and number:
  - Masculine singular: *menino alto* (tall boy).
  - Feminine singular: *menina alta* (tall girl).
  - Masculine plural: *meninos altos*.
  - Feminine plural: *meninas altas*.
- Some adjectives are invariable (e.g., *feliz* = happy → *menino feliz, menina feliz*).

Pronouns
- Subject pronouns:
  eu, tu, você, ele/ela, nós, vós, vocês, eles/elas.
  - *Tu* is used in Portugal and some regions of Brazil; *você* is more common in Brazil.
  - *O senhor / a senhora* = polite "you" (formal).
- Direct object pronouns: *me, te, o/a, nos, vos, os/as*.
- Indirect object pronouns: *me, te, lhe, nos, vos, lhes*.
- Reflexive pronouns: *me, te, se, nos, vos, se*.

Verbs
- Three main conjugation groups: **-ar, -er, -ir** (*falar, comer, partir*).
- Conjugations change by person, number, tense, and mood.
- Key moods:
  - **Indicative** (facts).
  - **Subjunctive** (doubt, wish, uncertainty).

- o **Imperative** (commands).
- Common tenses:
  - o **Present tense:** *eu falo* (I speak).
  - o **Preterite tense (simple past):** *eu falei* (I spoke).
  - o **Imperfect tense:** *eu falava* (I used to speak).
  - o **Future tense:** *eu falarei* (I will speak).
  - o **Conditional tense:** *eu falaria* (I would speak).
  - o Compound forms with **ter/haver:** *tenho falado* (I have spoken), *tinha falado* (I had spoken).
- Distinctive Feature: Portuguese often places object pronouns **after and attached to verbs** (*viu-me* = saw me), especially in European Portuguese.

Word Order
- Standard **SVO** (subject-verb-object): *Maria come pão* (Maria eats bread).
- Like Spanish, the subject can be dropped: *como pão* (I eat bread).
- More flexible in poetry and speech.

Questions and Negation
- Yes/No questions often use intonation: *Você fala português?* (You speak Portuguese?).
- No auxiliary verb like English "do."
- Negation: **não** before the verb (*Eu não falo inglês* = I don't speak English).

Prepositions
- Always used with pronouns in special forms: *para mim* (for me), *comigo* (with me), *contigo* (with you).
- Common ones: *a* (to), *de* (of/from), *em* (in/on), *com* (with), *por* (by/through), *para* (for/purpose).
- Prepositions often **contract with articles**:
  - o *de + o = do* (of the, masculine).
  - o *em + a = na* (in the, feminine).

Special Features
- **Ser vs. Estar** (both "to be"):
  - o *ser* = permanent qualities (*sou alto* = I am tall).
  - o *estar* = temporary states/locations (*estou cansado* = I am tired).
- **Saber vs. Conhecer** (both "to know"):
  - o *saber* = knowledge, facts (*sei a resposta* = I know the answer).
  - o *conhecer* = familiarity with people/places (*conheço Lisboa* = I know Lisbon).
- Double negatives are allowed and required (*não tenho nada* = I don't have anything).

Chapter III

French

The Lords Prayer in *Français* (French)

Notre Père

Notre Père, qui es aux cieux,
Que ton nom soit sanctifié,
Que ton règne vienne,
Que ta volonté soit faite sur la terre comme au ciel.
Donne-nous aujourd'hui notre pain de ce jour;
Pardonne-nous nos offenses,
Comme nous pardonnons aussi à ceux qui nous ont
offensés;
Et ne nous soumets pas à la tentation,
Mais délivre-nous du mal.
Amen.

<u>Word-to-Word Translation</u>

Notre Père *(The Our Father)*

Notre (Our) **Père,** (Father,)

qui (who) **es** (are) **aux** (in the) **cieux,** (heavens,)

Que (That) **ton** (your) **nom** (name) **soit** (be) **sanctifié,** (sanctified,)

Que (That) **ton** (your) **règne** (kingdom) **vienne,** (come,)

Que (That) **ta** (your) **volonté** (will) **soit** (be) **faite** (done),

sur (on) **la** (the) **terre** (earth) **comme** (as) **au** (in the) **ciel.** (heaven.)

Donne-nous (Give us) **aujourd'hui** (today) **notre** (our) **pain** (bread) **de** (of) **ce** (this) **jour;** (day;)

Pardonne-nous (Forgive us) **nos** (our) **offenses,** (offenses,)

Comme (As) **nous** (we) **pardonnons** (forgive) **aussi** (also) **à** (to) **ceux** (those) **qui** (who) **nous** (us) **ont** (have) **offensés ;** (offended;)

Et (And) **ne** (not) **nous** (us) **soumets** (submit) **pas** (not) **à** (to) **la** (the) **tentation,** (temptation,)

Mais (But) **délivre-nous** (deliver us) **du** (from the) **mal.** (evil.)

Amen. (Amen.)

Phonetic Pronunciation

Notre (noh-truh) Père (pehr)

Notre (noh-truh) Père (pehr),

qui (kee) es (eh) aux (oh) cieux (syuh),

que (kuh) ton (tohn) nom (noh) soit (swah) sanctifié (sank-tee-fee-ay);

que (kuh) ton (tohn) règne (regn) vienne (vyehn),

que (kuh) ta (tah) volonté (voh-lohn-tay) soit (swah) faite (fet),

sur (syur) la (lah) terre (tehr) comme (komm) au (oh) ciel (syel).

Donne (donn) nous (noo) aujourd'hui (oh-zhoor-dwee) notre (noh-truh) pain (pan) quotidien (ko-tee-dyan);

pardonne (par-donn) nos (no) offenses (oh-fahns),

comme (komm) nous (noo) pardonnons (par-donn-on) aussi (oh-see) à (ah) ceux (suh) qui (kee) nous (noo) ont (on) offensés (oh-fahn-say);

et (ay) ne (nuh) nous (noo) laisse (less) pas (pah) entrer (ahn-tray) en (ahn) tentation (tahn-ta-syohn),

mais (meh) délivre (day-leevr) nous (noo) du (du) mal (mal).

Amen (ah-men).

Understanding the French Alphabet

Alphabet

- French uses the standard Latin 26 letters: **A–Z**.
- Letters **K, W, Y** appear mainly in loanwords, names, or foreign terms.
- Alphabet order: … X, Y, Z.
- French does not treat digraphs as separate letters.

Letter Sounds Differ from English

- **A** = *ah* (chat = shah).
- **E** = can be open *eh* (mère = mehr) or closed *ay* (été = ay-tay).
- **I** = *ee* (lit = lee).
- **O** = *oh* or *aw* (porte = port; garçon = gar-sawn).
- **U** = fronted "ü" sound, lips rounded (lune ≈ lyoon).
- **É** = stressed, closed *e* (café = kah-fay).
- **J** = soft "zh" as in English *measure* (jamais = zhah-meh).
- **H** = always silent (homme = om).
- **R** = guttural, pronounced at the back of the throat.
- **C** = *k* before a, o, u; *s* before e, i (cat = cat / ceci = suh-see).
- **Ç** (cedilla) = *s* before a, o, u (garçon = gar-son).
- **X** = usually *ks* (taxi), sometimes *gz* (examen = eg-zah-men).
- **Y** = pronounced *ee* (lycée ≈ lee-say).
- **Double consonants**: pronounced normally; no strong doubling effect except for clarity.

Accent Marks

- **Acute (´)** → only on *é*, marks closed /e/ sound (café, réalité).
- **Grave (`)** → on *à, è, ù*, indicates open vowel or distinguishes words (père = father vs. pere = not a word).
- **Circumflex (ˆ)** → on *â, ê, î, ô, û*; often marks historical letter loss (hôpital from Latin *hospitalis*).
- **Cedilla (¸)** → under *ç*, makes C sound like *s* before a, o, u (garçon, ça).
- **Diaeresis (¨)** → on *ë, ï, ü*, indicates vowels are pronounced separately (Noël, naïf).

Understanding French Grammar

Nouns and Gender
- All nouns are either **masculine** (*le livre* = the book) or **feminine** (*la table* = the table).
- Gender often follows endings:
    o **-age, -ment, -eau, -isme** → usually masculine (*le fromage, le gouvernement*).
    o **-tion, -sion, -té, -ette, -ie** → usually feminine (*la nation, la liberté*).
- Plural: usually add **-s** (*livres*), but silent in speech unless followed by a vowel. Irregulars exist (*cheval* → *chevaux*).

Articles
- Definite: *le, la, l', les* = the.
- Indefinite: *un, une, des* = a, an, some.
- Partitive: *du, de la, de l', des* = some/any (*du pain* = some bread).
- Articles agree in gender and number with the noun.

Adjectives
- Usually placed **after** the noun (*une maison rouge* = a red house), but some come before (*un grand homme* = a great man).
- Must agree in gender and number:
    o Masculine singular: *petit* (small).
    o Feminine singular: *petite* (small).
    o Masculine plural: *petits* (small).
    o Feminine plural: *petites* (small).
- Some adjectives change form irregularly (*beau* → *bel, belle, beaux, belles*).

Pronouns
- Subject pronouns: *je, tu, il/elle/on, nous, vous, ils/elles*.
- Direct object pronouns: *me, te, le/la, nous, vous, les*.
- Indirect object pronouns: *me, te, lui, nous, vous, leur*.
- Reflexive pronouns: *me, te, se, nous, vous, se*.
- Stress (disjunctive) pronouns: *moi, toi, lui, elle, nous, vous, eux, elles*.
- French is **not a pro-drop language** → subject pronouns are required.

Verbs
- Three conjugation groups: **-er, -ir, -re** (*parler, finir, vendre*).
- Irregular verbs (être, avoir, aller, faire) are extremely common.
- Key tenses in the **indicative**:
    o **Present tense:** *je parle* (I speak).

- o **Past tense:** *j'ai parlé* (I spoke/have spoken).
- o **Imperfect tense:** *je parlais* (I was speaking/used to speak).
- o **Future simple tense:** *je parlerai* (I will speak).
- o **Conditional present tense:** *je parlerais* (I would speak).
- **Subjunctive** is frequent after expressions of doubt, desire, necessity (*il faut que tu viennes* = you must come).
- Compound tenses use **avoir** or **être** as auxiliaries: *je suis allé* (I am gone), *j'ai mangé* (I have eaten).

Word Order

- Standard **SVO** (subject-verb-object): *Marie mange du pain* (Marie eats bread).
- Adjectives usually **follow** the noun, except a small set that precede (*grand, petit, beau, vieux, bon, mauvais*).
- Pronoun placement: pronouns go **before** the verb (*je le vois* = I see it).

Questions and Negation

- Yes/No questions:
  - o Intonation: *Tu viens?* (You come?).
  - o *Est-ce que*: *Est-ce que tu viens?* (Is it that you come?).
  - o Inversion: *Viens-tu ?* (Come-you?).
- Negation: *ne … pas* around the verb (*je ne parle pas* = I don't speak).
- Variants: *ne … jamais* (never), *ne … rien* (nothing), *ne … personne* (nobody).
- In informal speech, *ne* is often dropped (*je parle pas* = I speak not).

Prepositions

- Common: *à* (to/at), *de* (of/from), *dans* (in), *avec* (with), *pour* (for), *par* (by).
- Contractions: *à + le = au, de + le = du*.
- Used with stress pronouns: *avec moi* (with me), *pour lui* (for him).

Special Features

- **Être vs. Avoir**: both auxiliary verbs; *être* used with movement verbs (*aller, venir, naître*).
- **Il y a** = there is/there are.
- **Partitive articles** are essential for talking about "some" or "any" (contrast with Spanish/Portuguese where bare nouns are used).
- **Agreement with past participles**: when used with *être* or when the direct object comes before the verb (*les filles que j'ai vues* = the girls I saw).

Chapter IV

Italian

The Lords Prayer in *Italiano* (Italian)

Il Padre Nostro

Padre nostro, che sei nei cieli,
sia santificato il tuo nome;
venga il tuo regno;
sia fatta la tua volontà,
come in cielo così in terra.
Dacci oggi il nostro pane quotidiano;
rimetti a noi i nostri debiti,
come noi li rimettiamo ai nostri debitori;
e non ci indurre in tentazione,
ma liberaci dal male.
Amen.

Word-to-Word Translation

Il Padre Nostro (The Our Father)

Padre (Father) **nostro** (our),

che (who) **sei** (are) **nei** (in the) **cieli** (heavens),

sia (may be) **santificato** (sanctified) **il** (the) **tuo** (your) **nome** (name);

venga (may come) **il** (the) **tuo** (your) **regno** (kingdom);

sia (may be) **fatta** (done) **la** (the) **tua** (your) **volontà** (will),

come (as) **in** (in) **cielo** (heaven) **così** (so) **in** (in) **terra** (earth).

Dacci (Give us) **oggi** (today) **il** (the) **nostro** (our) **pane** (bread) **quotidiano** (daily);

rimetti (forgive) **a** (to) **noi** (us) **i** (the) **nostri** (our) **debiti** (debts),

come (as) **noi** (we) **li** (them) **rimettiamo** (forgive) **ai** (to the) **nostri** (our) **debitori** (debtors);

e (and) **non** (not) **ci** (us) **indurre** (lead) **in** (into) **tentazione** (temptation),

ma (but) **liberaci** (deliver us) **dal** (from the) **male** (evil).

Amen (Amen).

Phonetic Pronunciation

Il Padre Nostro (Eel Pah-dreh Noh-stroh)

Padre (Pah-dreh) nostro (noh-stroh),

che (keh) sei (say) nei (nay) cieli (chyeh-lee),

sia (see-ah) santificato (sahn-tee-fee-kah-toh) il (eel) tuo (too-oh) nome (noh-meh);

venga (vehn-gah) il (eel) tuo (too-oh) regno (reh-nyoh);

sia (see-ah) fatta (faht-tah) la (lah) tua (too-ah) volontà, (voh-lohn-tah),

come (koh-meh) in (een) cielo (chyeh-loh) così (koh-zee) in (een) terra (tehr-rah).

Dacci (daht-chee) oggi (ohj-jee) il (eel) nostro (noh-stroh) pane (pah-neh) quotidiano (kwoh-tee-dee-ah-noh);

rimetti (ree-meht-tee) a (ah) noi (noy) i (ee) nostri (noh-stree) debiti (deh-bee-tee),

come (koh-meh) noi (noy) li (lee) rimettiamo (ree-meht-tyah-moh) ai (eye) nostri (noh-stree) debitori (deh-bee-toh-ree);

e (eh) non (nohn) ci (chee) indurre (een-door-reh) in (een) tentazione (tehn-tah-tsyoh-neh),

ma (mah) liberaci (lee-beh-rah-chee) dal (dahl) male (mah-leh).

Amen (ah-mehn).

Understanding the Italian Alphabet

Alphabet
- Italian uses the Latin alphabet with **21 core letters**.
- The letters **J, K, W, X, Y** are not native but appear in foreign words, names, and loanwords.
- Standard Italian letters: **A, B, C, D, E, F, G, H, I, L, M, N, O, P, Q, R, S, T, U, V, Z.**

Letter Sounds Differ from English
- **C before e, i** = *"ch"* as in *church* → *cielo* = *chee-eh-lo*.
- **C before a, o, u** = hard *k* → *casa* = *kah-sa*.
- **G before e, i** = soft *j* as in *gem* → *gelato* = *jeh-lah-to*.
- **G before a, o, u** = hard *g* → *gatto* = *gah-to*.
- **H** = always silent → *hotel* = *o-tel*.
- **R** = rolled or trilled.
- **S** = either *s* as in *see* or *z* as in *rose*.
- **Z** = *ts* (as in *pizza*) or *dz* (as in *zero*).
- **GL before i** = palatal *ly* sound → *famiglia* = *fa-mee-lya*.
- **GN** = palatal *ny* sound → *lasagna* = *la-zah-nya*.
- **Double consonants** = pronounced longer and can change meaning (*anno* = year vs. *ano* = anus).

Accent Marks
- **Grave (`)**: most common, shows stress on the last vowel → *città* (*chee-tà*), *però* (*pe-rò*).
- **Acute (´)**: mainly on *é*, distinguishes open vs. closed vowels → *perché* (*per-ké*).
- **Accent use**: distinguishes meaning → *e* (and) vs. *è* (is).
- Accents are usually written when stress falls on the **final syllable**; otherwise, stress is understood without marks.

Understanding Italian Grammar

Nouns and Gender
- All nouns are **masculine** (*il libro* = the book) or **feminine** (*la tavola* = the table).
- Gender often follows endings:
  - Masculine: *-o, -ore, -ma* (*ragazzo, dottore, problema*).
  - Feminine: *-a, -zione, -ice* (*ragazza, nazione, attrice*).
- Plural formation:
  - Masculine **-o** → **-i** (*libro* → *libri*).
  - Feminine **-a** → **-e** (*tavola* → *tavole*).
  - **-e** → **-i** regardless of gender (*cane* → *cani, notte* → *notti*).
  - Irregulars: *uomo* → *uomini, dio* → *dei*.

Articles
- **Definite** ("the"):
  - Masculine: *il, lo, l', i, gli*.
  - Feminine: *la, l', le*.
- **Indefinite** ("a, an"):
  - Masculine: *un, uno* (before s+consonant, z, gn, ps, x).
  - Feminine: *una, un'*.
- Articles agree in gender and number with the noun.

Adjectives
- Normally follow the noun (*una casa grande* = a big house).
- Some common ones precede (*un buon amico, una bella città*).
- Agreement patterns:
  - Masculine singular: *piccolo*.
  - Feminine singular: *piccola*.
  - Masculine plural: *piccoli*.
  - Feminine plural: *piccole*.
- Irregulars exist (*bello* → *bel, bello, begli, bella, belle*).

Pronouns
- Subject: *io, tu, lui/lei, noi, voi, loro*.
- Direct object: *mi, ti, lo/la, ci, vi, li/le*.
- Indirect object: *mi, ti, gli/le, ci, vi, loro*.
- Reflexive: *mi, ti, si, ci, vi, si*.
- Stressed (after prepositions): *me, te, lui/lei, noi, voi, loro*.
- Italian is a **pro-drop language**: subject pronouns often omitted (*Parlo* = I speak).

Italian ~ The Lords Prayer

Verbs
- Three conjugations: **-are, -ere, -ire** (*parlare, vedere, dormire*).
- Irregular verbs are common (*essere, avere, andare, fare, venire*).
- Key tenses:
  - **Present tense:** *parlo* (I speak).
  - **Past tense:** *ho parlato* (I spoke/have spoken).
  - **Imperfect tense:** *parlavo* (I was speaking/used to speak).
  - **Future tense:** *parlerò* (I will speak).
  - **Conditional present:** *parlerei* (I would speak).
- Compound tenses use *avere* or *essere*: *sono andato, ho mangiato*.

Word Order
- Standard **SVO** (subject-verb-object): *Maria mangia il pane* (Maria eats bread).
- Adjectives usually follow the noun, but placement can change meaning: *un uomo grande* (a big man) ≠ *un grande uomo* (a great man).
- Pronouns precede the verb (*lo vedo* = I see him/it).

Questions and Negation
- Yes/No questions use rising intonation (*Vieni?* = You come?) or inversion (*Viene Maria?* = Comes Maria?).
- Negation: *non* before the verb (*non parlo* = I don't speak).
- Other negatives: *mai* (never), *niente* (nothing), *nessuno* (nobody).

Prepositions
- Common: *a* (to/at), *di* (of/from), *in* (in), *con* (with), *per* (for), *da* (by/from), *su* (on).
- Prepositions often combine with articles: *a + il = al, di + il = del, in + la = nella*.
- Used with stressed pronouns: *con me, per lui*.

Special Features
- **Essere vs. Avere**: both auxiliaries; *essere* is used with motion and reflexive verbs (*sono arrivato, mi sono svegliato*).
- **C'è / Ci sono** = there is / there are.
- **Double negatives** are standard: *non ho visto nessuno* (I didn't see anyone).
- Agreement in compound tenses: with *essere* the participle agrees with the subject (*Maria è andata* = Maria is gone).

Chapter V

Dutch

The Lords Prayer in *Nederlands* (Dutch)

Onze Vader

Onze Vader, die in de hemelen zijt,
Uw naam worde geheiligd;
Uw koninkrijk kome;
Uw wil geschiede,
op de aarde zoals in de hemel;
Geef ons heden ons dagelijks brood;
en vergeef ons onze schulden,
zoals ook wij vergeven onze schuldenaren;
En leidt ons niet in verzoeking,
maar verlos ons van de boze.
Amen.

Word-to-Word Translation

Onze Vader *(The Our Father)*

Onze (Our) **Vader** (Father),

die (who) **in** (in) **de** (the) **hemelen** (heavens) **zijt** (are),

Uw (Your) **naam** (name) **worde** (be) **geheiligd** (sanctified),

Uw (Your) **koninkrijk** (kingdom) **kome** (come),

Uw (Your) **wil** (will) **geschiede** (be done),

op (on) **de** (the) **aarde** (earth) **gelijk** (as) **in** (in) **de** (the) **hemel** (heaven),

Geef (Give) **ons** (us) **heden** (today) **ons** (our) **dagelijks** (daily) **brood** (bread),

en (and) **vergeef** (forgive) **ons** (us) **onze** (our) **schulden** (debts),

gelijk (just as) **ook** (also) **wij** (we) **vergeven** (forgive) **onze** (our) **schuldenaren** (debtors);

En (And) **leid** (lead) **ons** (us) **niet** (not) **in** (into) **verzoeking** (temptation),

maar (but) **verlos** (deliver) **ons** (us) **van** (from) **de** (the) **boze** (evil).

Amen (Amen).

Phonetic Pronunciation

Onze Vader (On-zuh Vah-der)

Onze (on-zuh) **Vader** (vah-der),

die (dee) **in** (in) **de** (duh) **hemelen** (hay-meh-lun),

uw (uw) **naam** (nahm) **worde** (vor-duh) **geheiligd** (guh-hay-licht);

uw (uw) **koninkrijk** (koh-nink-rayk) **kome** (koh-muh);

uw (uw) **wil** (vil) **geschiede** (guh-schee-duh),

op (op) **de** (duh) **aarde** (ahr-duh) **gelijk** (guh-like) **in** (in) **de** (duh) **hemel** (hay-mul),

Geef (hayf) **ons** (ons) **heden** (hay-duhn) **ons** (ons) **dagelijks** (dah-ghuh-liks) **brood** (broht),

en (en) **vergeef** (ver-hayf) **ons** (ons) **onze** (on-zuh) **schulden** (skhul-duhn),

gelijk (guh-like) **ook** (ohk) **wij** (vay) **vergeven** (ver-hay-vun) **onze** (on-zuh) **schuldenaren** (skhul-duh-nah-ren),

en (en) **leid** (light) **ons** (ons) **niet** (neet) **in** (in) **verzoeking** (ver-zoo-king),

maar (mahr) **verlos** (ver-los) **ons** (ons) **van** (vahn) **de** (duh) **boze** (boh-zuh).

Amen (ah-men).

Understanding the Dutch Alphabet

Alphabet
- Dutch uses the standard 26 letters of the Latin alphabet (**A–Z**).
- The letters **Q, X, Y** are rare and mainly appear in names or foreign loanwords.
- The digraph **IJ** is often treated as a single unit in dictionaries and alphabetizing, though it consists of **I + J**.

Letter Sounds Differ from English
- **A** = usually *ah*, like in *father* (man = mahn).
- **E** = short *eh* (met = met), long *ay* (ze = zay), or schwa *uh* (de = duh).
- **I** = *ih* (lip = lip) or long *ee* (vier = feer).
- **O** = *oh* (bodem = boh-dem) or short *aw* (pot = pawt).
- **U** = rounded *u*, like French *u* or German *ü* (muur ≈ müür).
- **IJ / EI** = diphthong, like "ay" but more closed (ijs = ice).
- **OU / AU** = diphthong, like "ow" in *cow* (huis = house).
- **UI** = unique Dutch vowel, between "ow" and "eeu" (huis ≈ h-ow-ihs).
- **G / CH** = guttural, throaty "kh" sound, stronger than German *ch*.
- **J** = "y" in *yes* (jong = yohng).
- **K** = always hard *k* (kat = kaht).
- **W** = between English "v" and "w," lips rounded (water ≈ vah-ter).
- **V** = often like English *v*, but in some dialects closer to *f*.
- **Z** = usually *z*, but can sound closer to *s*.
- **R** = varies: rolled, tapped, or uvular depending on region.
- **Double consonants** = pronounced longer and can change meaning: *bellen* (to call) vs. *belen* (to donate).

Accent Marks
- Accents are rare; mainly used for emphasis or to distinguish words: *hé* (hey!) vs. *he* (he).
- Loanwords often retain original accents (*café, logé*).

Understanding Dutch Grammar

Nouns and Gender
- Dutch has **two genders** today: **common (de)** and **neuter (het)**.
- Historically masculine and feminine were separate, but now merged into common.
- Most nouns use **de**; short words and diminutives (*-je*) are usually **het** (*het huis, het meisje*).
- Plurals:
  - Add **-en** (*boek* → *boeken*).
  - Add **-s** if ending in a vowel (*auto* → *auto's*).
  - Spelling rules apply (double consonant, drop e, etc.).

Articles
- **Definite**: *de* (common), *het* (neuter), *de* (plural).
- **Indefinite**: *een* = a/an (no plural form).
- No partitive article like in French; *wat brood* = some bread.

Adjectives
- Normally precede the noun (*een groot huis* = a big house).
- Inflection:
  - With *de*-words and *het*-words when preceded by an article → add **-e** (*de grote man* = the big man, *het grote huis* = the big house).
  - Bare neuter singular → no **-e** (*een groot huis* = a big house).
- Some irregular forms: *goed* → *betere, best*.

Pronouns
- Subject: *ik, jij/je, u* (formal), *hij, zij/ze, het, wij/we, jullie, zij/ze*.
- Object: *mij/me, jou/je, u, hem, haar, het, ons, jullie, hen/ze*.
- Possessive: *mijn, jouw, uw, zijn, haar, ons/onze, jullie, hun*.
- Reflexive: *me, je, zich, ons, je, zich*.
- Dutch is a **pro-drop language only in imperatives**, otherwise subject pronouns are required (*Ik spreek Nederlands* = I speak Dutch).

Verbs
- Two main groups: **regular weak verbs** (*werken* → *werkte* → *gewerkt*) and **strong verbs** (with vowel change: *zien* → *zag* → *gezien*).
- Irregular verbs are common (*zijn, hebben, worden, gaan, doen*).

- Key tenses:
  - ○ **Present tense:** *ik spreek* (I speak).
  - ○ **Simple past tense:** *ik sprak* (I spoke).
  - ○ **Perfect tense:** *ik heb gesproken* (I have spoken).
  - ○ **Future tense:** *ik zal spreken* (I will speak).
  - ○ **Conditional tense:** *ik zou spreken* (I would speak).
- Compound tenses use *hebben* or *zijn*: *ik ben gegaan, ik heb gegeten*.

Word Order
- Standard **SVO** (subject-verb-object) in main clauses: (*Jan leest een boek* = Jan reads a book).
- Subordinate clauses: Verb goes to the end (*Ik weet dat Jan een boek leest* = I know that Jan reads a book).
- **V2 rule:** the verb is always second element in main clauses (*Vandaag leest Jan een boek* = Today reads Jan a book).
- Object and pronoun placement can shift depending on emphasis.

Questions and Negation
- Yes/No questions are inverted: *Lees jij het boek?* (Read you the book?).
- Negation: *niet* (not) or *geen* (no/none).
  - ○ *Ik spreek niet* = I don't speak.
  - ○ *Ik heb geen boek* = I have no book.

Prepositions
- Common: *in* (in), *op* (on), *bij* (at), *naar* (to), *met* (with), *van* (of/from), *voor* (for), *uit* (out of).
- Often form fixed phrases: *denken aan* (to think of), *houden van* (to love).
- Prepositions don't contract with articles as in French/Italian.

Special Features
- **Separable verbs:** prefix splits in main clauses (*ik neem deel* → *ik neem deel aan het spel*, but *ik deelneem aan het spel* in subordinate clause).
- **Double infinitives** appear in some constructions (*ik heb willen gaan* = I wanted to go).
- **Er** is multifunctional: place holder, existential (*er is een probleem*), quantity (*er zijn veel mensen*), or emphasis.
- Diminutives (*-je, -tje, -etje*) are extremely common and always neuter (*het huisje, het boompje*).

Chapter VI

Norwegian

The Lords Prayer in *Norsk* (Norwegian)

Vår Far

Vår Far, som er i himmelen,
la ditt navn holdes hellig,
la ditt rike komme,
la din vilje skje på jorden som i himmelen.
Gi oss i dag vårt daglige brød;
og forlat oss våre skyldner,
slik også vi forlater våre skyldnere;
og led oss ikke inn i fristelse,
men fri oss fra det onde.
Amen.

Word-to-Word Translation

Vår Far (The Our Father)

Vår (Our) **Far** (Father),

som (who) **er** (is) **i** (in) **himmelen** (the heaven),

la (let) **ditt** (your) **navn** (name) **holdes** (be kept) **hellig** (holy),

la (let) **ditt** (your) **rike** (kingdom) **komme** (come),

la (let) **din** (your) **vilje** (will) **skje** (happen) **på** (on) **jorden** (the earth) **som** (as) **i** (in) **himmelen** (the heaven).

Gi (Give) **oss** (us) **i** (in) **dag** (today) **vårt** (our) **daglige** (daily) **brød** (bread);

og (and) **forlat** (forgive) **oss** (us) **våre** (our) **skyldner** (debtors),

slik (as) **også** (also) **vi** (we) **forlater** (forgive) **våre** (our) **skyldnere** (debtors);

og (and) **led** (lead) **oss** (us) **ikke** (not) **inn** (into) **fristelse** (temptation),

men (but) **fri** (free) **oss** (us) **fra** (from) **det** (the) **onde** (evil).

Amen (Amen).

Phonetic Pronunciation

Vår (vor) Far (fahr)

Vår (vor) Far (fahr),

som (sohm) er (ehr) i (ee) himmelen (heem-meh-len),

la (lah) ditt (deet) navn (nahvn) holdes (hol-dess) hellig (hel-leeg),

la (lah) ditt (deet) rike (ree-keh) komme (koh-meh),

la (lah) din (deen) vilje (veel-yeh) skje (shyeh) på (paw) jorden (yor-den) som (sohm) i (ee) himmelen (heem-meh-len).

Gi (yee) oss (ohss) i (ee) dag (dahg) vårt (vawrt) daglige (dahg-lee-geh) brød (bruhd);

og (ohg) forlat (for-laht) oss (ohss) våre (vor-eh) skyldner (shild-ner),

slik (sleek) også (ohg-saw) vi (vee) forlater (for-lah-ter) våre (vor-eh) skyldnere (shild-neh-reh);

og (ohg) led (led) oss (ohss) ikke (ee-keh) inn (in) i (ee) fristelse (freest-leh-seh),

men (men) fri (free) oss (ohss) fra (frah) det (deh) onde (oon-deh).

Amen (ah-men).

Understanding the Norwegian Alphabet

Alphabet
- Norwegian has 29 letters: the standard Latin 26 (**A–Z**) plus **Æ, Ø, Å**, which are considered distinct letters.
- Alphabet order: … X, Y, Z, Æ, Ø, Å.
- Letters **C, Q, W, X, Z** are rare and mostly used in names, foreign words, or older spellings.

Letter Sounds Differ from English
- **Æ** = like *a* in *cat* (næ = nah).
- **Ø** = like French *peur* or German *ö*, a rounded "er" sound (bøk = bœk).
- **Å** = like "aw" in *law* (gård = gawrd).
- **A** = usually *ah*, shorter in some words (mann = mahnn).
- **E** = can be long *eh* (se = seh, see) or short (ett = eht).
- **I** = *ee* in *machine* (vit = veet).
- **O** = varies: *oo* (ord = oord) or *oh* (sol = sool).
- **U** = between English *oo* and German *ü* (hus ≈ hüs).
- **Y** = fronted "ee" sound, like German ü (ny = nü).
- **J** = "y" as in *yes* (jeg = yay).
- **K before i, y (and sometimes e)** = "sh/ch" in Eastern Norwegian (kjempe = shem-pe); hard *k* elsewhere (katt = kaht).
- **G before i, y, e** = soft "y" (geit = yite); hard elsewhere (god = good).
- **H** = pronounced at the start of words, silent before j and v (hjelp = yelp).
- **SK / SJ** before front vowels = deep "sh/hw" sound (skjema ≈ shay-ma).
- **V** = like English *v*, sometimes close to *w*.
- **W** = between *v* and *w*, mostly in names and foreign words (Washington).
- **Z** = usually *s*, sometimes *z* depending on region.
- **R** = rolled or tapped in most dialects, uvular in some urban varieties.
- **Double consonants** = lengthened, which can change meaning: *mann* = man vs. *man* = singular indefinite.

Accent Marks
- Rare in native words; sometimes used to distinguish homonyms: *for* vs. *fór* (went).
- Loanwords often retain original accents (*idé, kafé*).
- Norwegian has **two pitch accents** (like Swedish, not written), which distinguish meaning in some dialects: *bønder* = farmers vs. *bønner* = beans.

Understanding Norwegian Grammar

Nouns and Gender
- Norwegian has **three genders**: masculine, feminine, neuter.
  - Masculine is most common (*en bil* = a car).
  - Feminine is optional in Bokmål (can be treated as masculine: *ei bok* / *en bok* = a book).
  - Neuter: *et hus* = a house.
- Plurals:
  - Masculine: (*-er*) *en bil* → *biler* (a car → cars).
  - Feminine: (*-er*) *ei bok* → *bøker* (a book → books).
  - Neuter: (*-er*) or no ending *et hus* → *hus* (a house → houses).
- Definite form is suffixed to the noun: *bil* → *bilen* (the car), *bok* → *boka/boken* (the book), *hus* → *huset* (the house).

Articles
- **Indefinite**: *en* (m.), *ei* (f.), *et* (n.).
- **Definite (suffixed)**: *-en, -a, -et*.
- With adjectives, a separate definite article *den/det/de* is used: *den store bilen* (the big car).

Adjectives
- Normally precede nouns: *et stort hus* = a big house.
- Inflection:
  - Masculine/Feminine singular: *stor*.
  - Neuter singular: *stort*.
  - Plural/Definite: *store*.
- Some irregular forms (*liten* → *lita/lite/små*).

Pronouns
- Subject: *jeg, du, han, hun, det, den, vi, dere, de*.
- Object: *meg, deg, ham/han, henne, det, den, oss, dere, dem*.
- Possessive: *min/mitt/mine, din/ditt/dine, hans, hennes, vår/vårt/våre, deres, sin/sitt/sine*.
- Reflexive: *seg*.
- Norwegian is **not pro-drop**: subjects are required (*Jeg snakker norsk* = I speak Norwegian).

Verbs
- No person conjugation (same form for all subjects).
- Two main groups: **weak verbs** (*snakke* → *snakket* → *har snakket*) and **strong verbs** (*skrive* → *skrev* → *har skrevet*).

- Irregular verbs: *være* (to be), *ha* (to have), *gjøre* (to do), *gå* (to go).
- Key tenses:
  o **Present tense**: *jeg snakker* (I speak).
  o **Preterite tense**: *jeg snakket* (I spoke).
  o **Perfect tense**: *jeg har snakket* (I have spoken).
  o **Future tense**: *jeg skal/vil snakke* (I will speak).
  o **Conditional tense**: *jeg ville snakke* (I would speak).
- Compound tenses are formed with *ha* or *være*.

Word Order

- Standard **SVO** (subject-verb-object) in main clauses: *Han leser en bok* (He is reading a book).
- **V2 rule**: verb must be second element: *I dag leser han en bok* (Today he is reading a book).
- Subordinate clauses: verb goes to the end: *Jeg vet at han leser en bok* (I know that he is reading a book).
- Negation (*ikke*) comes after the verb in main clauses: *Jeg snakker ikke norsk* (I don't speak Norwegian).

Questions and Negation

- Yes/No questions are inverted: *Snakker du norsk?* (Speak you Norwegian?).
- Question words: *hva* (what), *hvem* (who), *hvor* (where), *når* (when), *hvorfor* (why), *hvordan* (how).
- Negation: *ikke* (not). *Jeg spiser ikke kjøtt* = I don't eat meat.

Prepositions

- Common: *i* (in), *på* (on/at), *til* (to), *fra* (from), *med* (with), *om* (about), *for* (for).
- Often used in idiomatic expressions (*å være glad i* = to be fond of).

Special Features

- Definite suffixes on nouns are a hallmark of Norwegian (*bok* → *boka/boken*).
- Double definiteness: definite article + suffixed definite when adjective is used (*den store bilen*).
- Modal verbs (*skal, vil, kan, må, bør*) are common and followed by bare infinitives.
- Close similarity with Danish and Swedish means mutual intelligibility.

Chapter VII

Swedish

The Lords Prayer in *Svenska* (Swedish)

Fader vårnze

Fader vår, som är i himmelen.
Helgat varde ditt namn.
Tillkomme ditt rike.
Ske din vilja, såsom i himmelen,
så ock på jorden.
Vårt dagliga bröd giv oss idag.
Och förlåt oss våra skulder,
såsom ock vi förlåta dem oss skyldiga äro.
Och inled oss icke i frestelse,
utan fräls oss ifrån ondo.
Ty riket är ditt, och makten och härligheten i
evighet.
Amen.

Word-to-Word Translation

Fader vår (The Our Father)

Fader (Father) vår,(our),

som (who) är (are) i (in) himmelen (heaven),

helgat (hallowed) blive (be) ditt (your) namn (name);

tillkomme (come) ditt (your) rike (kingdom);

ske (be done) din (your) vilja (will),

såsom (as) i (in) himmelen (heaven) så (so) ock (also) på (on) jorden (earth);

Vårt (our) dagliga (daily) bröd (bread) giv (give) oss (us) idag (today);

och (and) förlåt (forgive) oss (us) våra (our) skulder (debts),

såsom (as) ock (also) vi (we) förlåta (forgive) dem (them) oss (us) skyldiga (indebted) äro (are);

Och (and) inled (lead) oss (us) icke (not) i (into) frestelse (temptation),

utan (but) fräls (deliver) oss (us) ifrån (from) ondo (evil).

Amen (Amen).

Phonetic Pronunciation

Fader vår (Fah-dehr vohr)

Fader (Fah-dehr) **vår** (vohr),

som (sohm) **är** (ahr) **i** (ee) **himmelen** (heem-meh-len),

helgat (hel-gaht) **blive** (blee-veh) **ditt** (deet) **namn** (nahm);

tillkomme (til-kom-meh) **ditt** (deet) **rike** (ree-keh);

ske (skeh) **din** (deen) **vilja** (veel-yah),

såsom (soh-som) **i** (ee) **himmelen** (heem-meh-len) **så** (soh) **ock** (ohk) **på** (poh) **jorden** (yor-den);

Vårt (vohrt) **dagliga** (dah-glee-gah) **bröd** (bruhd) **giv** (giv) **oss** (ohs) **idag** (ee-dahg);

och (ohk) **förlåt** (fer-loht) **oss** (ohs) **våra** (voh-rah) **skulder** (skool-der),

såsom (soh-som) **ock** (ohk) **vi** (vee) **förlåta** (fer-loh-tah) **dem** (dem) **oss** (ohs) **skyldiga** (skil-dee-gah) **äro** (air-oh);

Och (ohk) **inled** (in-led) **oss** (ohs) **icke** (ee-keh) **i** (ee) **frestelse** (fres-tel-seh),

utan (oo-tahn) **fräls** (frels) **oss** (ohs) **ifrån** (ee-frawn) **ondo** (on-doh);

Amen (ah-men).

Understanding the Swedish Alphabet

Alphabet
- Swedish has 29 letters: the standard Latin 26 (**A–Z**) plus **Å, Ä, Ö**, which are considered distinct letters, not just variants.
- Alphabet order: … X, Y, Z, Å, Ä, Ö.
- Letters **Q, W, Z** are rare and mainly appear in names or older/foreign words.

Letter Sounds Differ from English
- **Å** = like "aw" in *law* (gård = gawrd).
- **Ä** = like "a" in *cat* (här = hair).
- **Ö** = like French *peur* or German *ö* (söt = sûr-t).
- **A** = usually *ah*, but shorter in some words (land = lahnd).
- **E** = long *eh* (se = seh, see) or short (ett = eht).
- **I** = long *ee* in machine (vit = veet).
- **O** = can sound like *oo* (ord = oord) or *oh* (sol = sool).
- **U** = unique Swedish vowel, between French *u* and German *ü* (hus ≈ hüs).
- **Y** = fronted *ee* sound, like German *ü* (ny = nü).
- **J** = "y" as in *yes* (ja = yah).
- **K before i, e, ä, ö, y** = "sh/ch" (kyrka = shür-ka); hard *k* elsewhere (katt = kaht).
- **G before i, e, ä, ö, y** = "y" (ge = yeh); hard *g* elsewhere (god = good).
- **H** = pronounced at the beginning of words, silent before j and v (hjärta = yair-ta).
- **SK / SJ / STJ / RS** before front vowels = breathy "sh/hw" sound (sjö ≈ h-shuh).
- **V** = like English *v*, sometimes close to *w*.
- **R** = trilled or tapped in many dialects, uvular in others.
- **Double consonants** = lengthened: *manna* (man-na) vs. *mana* (mah-na).

Accent Marks
- Rare in native words; mainly used in loanwords (*idé, café*).
- Swedish also has **two pitch accents** (not written, but heard), which can change meaning: *anden* (the duck) vs. *anden* (the spirit).

Understanding Swedish Grammar

Nouns and Gender
- Swedish has **two genders**:
    - **Common (en-words)**, combining masculine and feminine (*en bok* = a book).
    - **Neuter (ett-words)** (*ett hus* = a house).
- Definite form is suffixed: *bok* → *boken* (the book), *hus* → *huset* (the house).
- Plural forms vary by gender and word class:
    - *en bok* → *böcker* (a book → books).
    - *ett hus* → *hus* (a house → houses).
    - *en bil* → *bilar* (a car → cars).

Articles
- **Indefinite**: *en* (common), *ett* (neuter).
- **Definite (suffixed)**: *-en, -et, -n, -t, -a*.
- With adjectives, a separate definite article *den/det/de* is used: *den stora bilen* (the big car).

Adjectives
- Normally placed before the noun: *ett rött hus* = a red house.
- Inflect for gender, number, and definiteness:
    - Common singular: *stor* (big).
    - Neuter singular: *stort* (big).
    - Plural/Definite: *stora* (big).
- Irregular forms exist (*liten* → *litet* → *små*).

Pronouns
- Subject: *jag, du, han, hon, den, det, vi, ni, de.*
- Object: *mig, dig, honom, henne, den, det, oss, er, dem.*
- Possessive: *min/mitt/mina, din/ditt/dina, hans, hennes, vår/vårt/våra, er/ert/era, deras, sin/sitt/sina.*
- Reflexive: *sig.*
- Swedish is **not pro-drop**: subjects are required (*Jag talar svenska* = I speak Swedish).

Verbs
- Verbs do not conjugate for person or number.
- Four main conjugation groups, weak and strong.
- Common irregulars: *vara* (to be), *ha* (to have), *göra* (to do), *gå* (to go).
- Key tenses:

- o **Present tense**: *jag talar* (I speak).
- o **Preterite tense**: *jag talade* (I spoke).
- o **Perfect tense**: *jag har talat* (I have spoken).
- o **Future tense**: *jag ska tala* (I will speak).
- o **Conditional tense**: *jag skulle tala* (I would speak).
- Compound tenses formed with *ha* or *vara*.

Word Order

- Standard **SVO** (subject-verb-object): *Han läser en bok* (He reads a book).
- **V2 rule**: the verb must be second: *Idag läser han en bok* (Today he reads a book).
- Subordinate clauses: verb moves later (*Jag vet att han läser en bok* = I know that he reads a book).
- Negation (*inte*) follows the verb in main clauses (*Jag talar inte svenska* = I do not speak Swedish).

Questions and Negation

- Yes/No questions are inverted: *Talar du svenska?* (Speak you Swedish?).
- Question words: *vad* (what), *vem* (who), *var* (where), *när* (when), *varför* (why), *hur* (how).
- Negation: *inte* (not). *Jag äter inte kött* = I don't eat meat.

Prepositions

- Common: *i* (in), *på* (on/at), *till* (to), *från* (from), *med* (with), *om* (about), *för* (for).
- Often idiomatic: *att vara kär i* = to be in love with.

Special Features

- Definite suffixes on nouns mark "the" (*bok → boken*).
- Double definiteness: definite article + suffixed definite when an adjective is used (*den stora boken*).
- Modal verbs (*ska, vill, kan, måste, bör*) take bare infinitives.
- Very close to Norwegian and fairly mutually intelligible.

Chapter VIII

Danish

The Lords Prayer in *Dansk* (Danish)

Fadervor

Fader vor, du som er i himlene!
Helliget blive dit navn,
komme dit rige,
ske din vilje,
som i himlen, således også på jorden;
giv os i dag vort daglige brød,
og forlad os vor skyld,
som også vi forlader vore skyldnere;
og led os ikke ind i fristelse,
men fri os fra det onde.
Amen.

Word-to-Word Translation

Fadervor (The Our Father)

Fadervor, (Our Father,)

du (you) **som** (who) **er** (are) **i** (in) **himlene** (the heavens),

Helliget (hallowed) **blive** (be) **dit** (your) **navn,** (name,)

komme (come) **dit** (your) **rige,** (kingdom,)

ske (be done) **din** (your) **vilje,** (will,)

som (as) **i** (in) **himlen** (the heaven) **således** (so) **også** (also) **på** (on) **jorden.** (the earth.)

Giv (give) **os** (us) **i** (in) **dag** (today) **vort** (our) **daglige** (daily) **brød,** (bread,)

og (and) **forlad** (forgive) **os** (us) **vor** (our) **skyld,** (guilt,)

som (as) **også** (also) **vi** (we) **forlader** (forgive) **vore** (our) **skyldnere.** (debtors.)

Led (lead) **os** (us) **ikke** (not) **ind** (into) **fristelse,** (temptation,)

men (but) **fri** (free) **os** (us) **fra** (from) **det** (the) **onde.** (evil.)

Amen. (Amen.)

Phonetic Pronunciation

Fadervor (Fah-der-vor)

Fadervor, (Fah-der-vor)

du (doo) **som** (sohm) **er** (air) **i** (ee) **himlene** (heem-leh-neh),

Helliget (hel-li-eth) **blive** (blee-veh) **dit** (deet) **navn** (nahvn),

komme (kom-meh) **dit** (deet) **rige** (ree-eh),

ske (skeh) **din** (deen) **vilje** (veel-yeh),

som (sohm) **i** (ee) **himlen** (heem-len) **således** (soh-lehs) **også** (aw-saw) **på** (poh) **jorden** (yor-den).

Giv (gee-veh) **os** (oss) **i** (ee) **dag** (dah) **vort** (vohrt) **daglige** (dahg-lee-eh) **brød** (bruhð),

og (oh) **forlad** (for-lath) **os** (oss) **vor** (vohr) **skyld** (skuhl),

som (sohm) **også** (aw-saw) **vi** (vee) **forlader** (for-lay-ther) **vore** (voh-reh) **skyldnere** (skuhl-neh-reh).

Led (lehl) **os** (oss) **ikke** (ee-keh) **ind** (een) **fristelse** (fris-teh-leh-seh),

men (men) **fri** (free) **os** (oss) **fra** (fra) **det** (deh) **onde** (oh-neh).

Amen. (Ah-men)

Understanding the Danish Alphabet

Alphabet
- Danish has 29 letters: the standard Latin 26 (**A–Z**) plus **Æ, Ø, Å**, which are considered distinct letters.
- Alphabet order: … X, Y, Z, Æ, Ø, Å.
- Letters **C, Q, W, X, Z** are rare and mostly appear in names, foreign words, or older spellings.

Letter Sounds Differ from English
- **Æ** = like "a" in *cat* (sæt = set).
- **Ø** = like French *peur* or German *ö* (børn = bœrn).
- **Å** = like "aw" in *law* (gård = gawrd).
- **A** = usually *ah*, shorter in unstressed syllables (mand = mahnd).
- **E** = can be short *eh* (men = men) or schwa-like *uh* in unstressed syllables (det = deh).
- **I** = long *ee* (vind = veend) or short *ih* (sit = sit).
- **O** = rounded *oh* (god = goh) or short *aw* (pot = pawt).
- **U** = close rounded *oo* (hus = hoos).
- **Y** = fronted *ee* sound like German ü (ny = nü).
- **J** = "y" as in *yes* (jeg = yay).
- **K before i, e, y, æ, ø** = soft palatal *sh/ch* in some dialects (kærlighed ≈ shær-lee-hed); hard *k* elsewhere (kat = kaht).
- **G before i, e, y, æ, ø** = soft "y" (geit ≈ yite); hard elsewhere (god = good).
- **H** = pronounced at the start of words, silent before j (hjælp = yelp).
- **R** = guttural or uvular in standard Danish, sometimes trilled in regional dialects.
- **V** = like English *v*, sometimes softer.
- **W** = mainly in loanwords and names (Washington).
- **Z** = mainly in loanwords (zoo = zoo).
- **Double consonants** = lengthened and can affect meaning: *mannen* (the man) vs. *manen* (the moon).

Accent Marks
- Rare in native words; sometimes used in loanwords (*idé, café*).
- **Acute accent (´)** marks stress or distinguishes words: *fór* (went) vs. *for* (for).
- Danish also has **stød**, a glottal or creaky-voice feature (not written) that distinguishes some words: *bønder* (farmers) vs. *bønner* (beans).

Understanding Danish Grammar

Nouns and Gender
- Danish has **two genders**:
    - **Common (n-words)** (*en bog* = a book).
    - **Neuter (t-words)** (*et hus* = a house).
- Definite form is suffixed: *bog* → *bogen* (the book), *hus* → *huset* (the house).
- Plural forms:
    - Common: add **-er** or **-e** (*en bil* → *biler*).
    - Neuter: often add **-e** (*et hus* → *huse*).

Articles
- **Indefinite**: *en* (common), *et* (neuter).
- **Definite (suffixed)**: *-en, -et, -n, -t*.
- With adjectives, a separate definite article *den/ det/ de* is used: *den store bog* (the big book).

Adjectives
- Normally precede nouns: *et stort hus* = a big house.
- Inflect for gender, number, and definiteness:
    - Common singular: *stor*.
    - Neuter singular: *stort*.
    - Plural/Definite: *store*.
- Irregular forms exist (*lille* → *lille/ lille/ små*).

Pronouns
- Subject: *jeg, du, han, hun, den, det, vi, I, de*.
- Object: *mig, dig, ham, hende, den, det, os, jer, dem*.
- Possessive: *min/ mit/ mine, din/ dit/ dine, hans, hendes, vores, jeres, deres, sin/ sit/ sine*.
- Reflexive: *sig*.
- Danish is **not pro-drop**: subjects are required (*Jeg taler dansk*).

Verbs
- Verbs do not conjugate for person or number.
- Four main conjugation groups, weak and strong.
- Irregulars: *være* (to be), *have* (to have), *gøre* (to do), *gå* (to go).
- Key tenses:
    - **Present tense**: *jeg taler* (I speak).
    - **Preterite tense**: *jeg talte* (I spoke).
    - **Perfect tense**: *jeg har talt* (I have spoken).
    - **Future tense**: *jeg vil tale* (I will speak).

- ○ **Conditional tense**: *jeg ville tale* (I would speak).
- ○ Compound tenses formed with *have* or *være*.

Word Order
- Standard **SVO** (subject-verb-object): *Han læser en bog* (He reads a book).
- **V2 rule**: verb must be second element *I dag læser han en bog* (Today he reads a book).
- Subordinate clauses: verb moves to the end *Jeg ved, at han læser en bog* (I know that he reads a book).
- Negation (*ikke*) comes after the verb: *Jeg taler ikke dansk* (I do not speak Danish).

Questions and Negation
- Yes/No questions are inverted: *Taler du dansk?* (Speak you Danish?).
- Question words: *hvad* (what), *hvem* (who), *hvor* (where), *hvornår* (when), *hvorfor* (why), *hvordan* (how).
- Negation: *ikke* (not). *Jeg spiser ikke kød* = I don't eat meat.

Prepositions
- Common: *i* (in), *på* (on/at), *til* (to), *fra* (from), *med* (with), *om* (about), *for* (for).
- Often idiomatic: *at være glad for* = to be fond of.

Special Features
- Definite suffixes mark "the" (*bog* → *bogen*).
- Double definiteness: definite article + suffixed definite when an adjective is used (*den store bog*).
- Modal verbs (*skal, vil, kan, må, bør*) take bare infinitives.
- Closely related to Norwegian and Swedish, with some pronunciation differences affecting mutual intelligibility.

Chapter IX

Romanian

The Lords Prayer in *Română* (Romanian)

Tatăl Nostru

Tatăl nostru, care eşti în ceruri,
sfinţească-se numele Tău,
vină împărăţia Ta,
facă-se voia Ta,
precum în cer aşa şi pe pământ.
Pâinea noastră cea de toate zilele
dă-ne-o nouă astăzi,
şi ne iartă nouă greşelile noastre,
precum şi noi iertăm greşiţilor noştri,
şi nu ne duce pe noi în ispită,
ci ne izbăveşte de cel rău.
Amin.

Romanian ~ The Lords Prayer

Word-to-Word Translation

Tatăl nostru (The Our Father)

Tatăl (Father) nostru, (our,)

care (who) eşti (are) în (in) ceruri, (heavens,)

sfinţească-se (hallowed be) numele (the name) Tău, (your,)

vină (come) împărăţia (the kingdom) Ta, (your,)

facă-se (be done) voia (the will) Ta, (your,)

precum (as) în (in) cer (heaven) aşa (so) şi (also) pe (on) pământ.
(earth.)

Pâinea (the bread) noastră (our) cea (the) de (of) toate (all) zilele
(days)

dă-ne-o (give us it) nouă (to us) astăzi, (today,)

şi (and) ne (to us) iartă (forgive) nouă (us) greşelile (the mistakes)
noastre,

(our,) precum (as) şi (also) noi (we) iertăm (forgive) greşiţilor (the
sinners) noştri, (our,)

şi (and) nu (not) ne (us) duce (lead) pe (into) noi (us) în (in) ispită,
(temptation,)

ci (but) ne (us) izbăveşte (deliver) de (from) cel (the) rău. (evil.)

Amin. (Amen.)

Phonetic Pronunciation

Tatăl nostru (TAH-tuhl NOHS-troo)

Tatăl (TAH-tuhl) nostru (NOHS-troo),

care (KAH-reh) eşti (yesht) în (uhn) ceruri (CHEH-roor),

sfinţească-se (sfeen-TSAHS-koo-seh) numele (NOO-meh-leh)
Tău (Tuh-oo),

vină (VEE-nuh) împărăţia (uhm-puh-ruh-TSEE-ah) Ta (Tah),

facă-se (FAH-kuh-seh) voia (VOY-ah) Ta (Tah),

precum (preh-KOOM) în (uhn) cer (cher) aşa (ah-SHAH) şi (shee)
pe (peh) pământ (puh-MUhnt).

Pâinea (PUI-nyah) noastră (NOH-ahs-trah) cea (chah) de (deh)
toate (TWAH-teh) zilele (ZEE-leh-leh)

dă-ne-o (DUH-neh-oh) nouă (NOH-oo-eh) astăzi (AH-stahz),

şi (shee) ne (neh) iartă (YAR-tuh) nouă (NOH-oo-eh) greşelile
(greh-SHEH-lee-leh) noastre (NOH-ahs-treh),

precum (preh-KOOM) şi (shee) noi (noy) iertăm (yer-TAHM)
greşiţilor (greh-SHEE-tsee-lor) noştri (NOSH-tree),

şi (shee) nu (noo) ne (neh) duce (DOO-cheh) pe (peh) noi (noy) în
(uhn) ispită (ees-PEE-tuh),

ci (chee) ne (neh) izbăveşte (eez-buh-VEHsh-teh) de (deh) cel
(chel) rău (ruh-oo).

Amin. (Ah-MEEN)

Understanding the Romanian Alphabet

Alphabet
- Romanian uses the Latin alphabet with **31 letters**, including five special characters: **Ă, Â, Î, Ș, Ț**.
- Alphabet order: … X, Y, Z, Ă, Â, Î, Ș, Ț.
- Letters **Q, W, K, Y** appear mostly in loanwords, foreign names, and older spellings.

Letter Sounds Differ from English
- **Ă** = mid-central vowel, like *uh* in *sofa* (măr = m-uh-r).
- **Â / Î** = close central vowel, roughly between English *uh* and *i* (în = î-n).
- **Ș** = *sh* as in *shoe* (șarpe = shar-pe).
- **Ț** = *ts* as in *cats* (țară = tsah-rah).
- **A** = *ah* (casă = kah-suh).
- **E** = *eh* (ele = eh-leh).
- **I** = *ee* (miel = meel).
- **O** = *oh* (om = ohm).
- **U** = *oo* (lup = loop).
- **J** = *zh* as in *measure* (jar = zhar).
- **C before e, i** = *ch* as in *church* (ce = cheh).
- **C before a, o, u** = hard *k* (casă = kah-suh).
- **G before e, i** = *j* as in *gem* (ger = jehr).
- **G before a, o, u** = hard *g* (gând = gahnd).
- **H** = always pronounced (hotel = ho-tel).
- **R** = rolled or trilled.
- **V** = like English *v*.
- **Z** = like English *z*.
- **Double consonants** = pronounced normally; no strong doubling effect.

Accent Marks
- **Ă, Â, Î, Ș, Ț** function as distinct letters and indicate pronunciation.
- Romanian also uses **acute (´) or circumflex (ˆ) in loanwords** for stress or clarity: *école, hârtie*.
- Stress is generally **not marked**, but falls usually on the penultimate syllable.

Understanding Romanian Grammar

Nouns and Gender
- Romanian has **three genders**: masculine, feminine, neuter.
- Neuter nouns behave like masculine in the singular and feminine in the plural: *un birou → birouri* (a desk → desks)
- Definite article is **enclitic** (added at the end):
    - Masculine: *băiat → băiatul* (boy → the boy).
    - Feminine: *fată → fata* (girl → the girl).
    - Neuter: *birou → biroul* (desk → the desk).
- Plurals differ by gender:
    - Masculine: *(-i) băiat → băieți* (boy → boys)
    - Feminine: *(-e) fată → fete* (girl → girls)
    - Neuter: like masculine in plural *(birou → birouri)*.

Articles
- **Indefinite**: *un* (m.), *o* (f.), *un* (n. neuter singular).
- **Definite**: enclitic as above.
- Articles agree with gender and number.

Adjectives
- Usually follow nouns *(carte frumoasă* = beautiful book), but can precede for emphasis *(frumoasa carte)*.
- Must agree in gender, number, and definiteness:
    - Masculine singular: *frumos*.
    - Feminine singular: *frumoasă*.
    - Plural: *frumoși* (m.), *frumoase* (f. & neut.).

Pronouns
- Subject: *eu, tu, el, ea, noi, voi, ei, ele*.
- Object: *mă, te, îl, o, ne, vă, îi, le*.
- Possessive: *meu, mea, mei, mele* (agree in gender and number).
- Reflexive: *se*.
- Romanian is **not pro-drop**, though subject pronouns are often omitted because verb endings indicate the subject.

Verbs
- Three conjugation groups based on infinitive endings: *-a, -e, -i*.
- Irregular verbs are common: *a fi* (to be), *a avea* (to have), *a face* (to do/make).
- Key tenses:
    - **Present tense**: *eu vorbesc* (I speak).

- o **Compound perfect**: *am vorbit* (I have spoken/I spoke).
- o **Imperfect tense**: *vorbeam* (I was speaking/used to speak).
- o **Future tense**: *voi vorbi* (I will speak).
- o **Conditional tense**: *aş vorbi* (I would speak).
- Subjunctive used after verbs of desire, necessity, or doubt: *să vină* (that he/she come).

Word Order
- Standard **SVO** (subject-verb-object): *Maria mănâncă pâine* (Maria eats bread).
- Adjectives usually follow the noun, except for stylistic/emphatic placement.
- Pronouns: object pronouns usually precede the verb (*Îl văd* = I see him).

Questions and Negation
- Yes/No questions can be formed in either intonation (raising your pitch at the end) or *oare: Maria vine? Oare vine Maria?* (Is Maria coming?).
- Question words: *ce* (what), *cine* (who), *unde* (where), *când* (when), *de ce* (why), *cum* (how).
- Negation: *nu* before the verb (*Nu vorbesc româneşte* = I don't speak Romanian).

Prepositions
- Common: *la* (at/to), *de* (of/from), *în* (in), *cu* (with), *pentru* (for), *pe* (on/for).
- Often combined with articles: *la + el = la el* (at him), *de + o = de o* (of a).

Special Features
- Definite article **suffix on the noun** is unique among Romance languages (*carte → cartea*).
- Neuter gender acts like masculine in singular, feminine in plural.
- Partitive sense expressed with *un/ nişte* (*un pic de apă* = a little water).
- Verb endings indicate person and number, allowing omission of subject pronouns in many cases.

Chapter X

German

The Lords Prayer in *Deutsch* (German)

Das Vaterunser

Vater unser, der du bist im Himmel,
geheiligt werde dein Name.
Dein Reich komme.
Dein Wille geschehe,
wie im Himmel so auf Erden.
Unser tägliches Brot gib uns heute.
Und vergib uns unsere Schuld,
wie auch wir vergeben unsern Schuldigern.
Und führe uns nicht in Versuchung,
sondern erlöse uns von dem Bösen.
Amen.

Word-to-Word Translation

Das Vaterunser (The Our Father)

Vater unser, (Father our,)

der (who) **du** (you) **bist** (are) **im** (in the) **Himmel,** (heaven,)

geheiligt (hallowed) **werde** (become) **dein** (your) **Name.** (name.)

Dein (your) **Reich** (kingdom) **komme.** (come.)

Dein (your) **Wille** (will) **geschehe,** (be done,)

wie (as) **im** (in the) **Himmel** (heaven) **so** (so) **auf** (on) **Erden.** (earth.)

Unser (our) **tägliches** (daily) **Brot** (bread) **gib** (give) **uns** (us) **heute.** (today.)

Und (and) **vergib** (forgive) **uns** (us) **unsere** (our) **Schuld,** (guilt,)

wie (as) **auch** (also) **wir** (we) **vergeben** (forgive) **unsern** (our) **Schuldigern.** (debtors.)

Und (and) **führe** (lead) **uns** (us) **nicht** (not) **in** (into) **Versuchung,** (temptation,)

sondern (but) **erlöse** (deliver) **uns** (us) **von** (from) **dem** (the) **Bösen.** (evil.)

Amen. (Amen.)

Phonetic Pronunciation

Das Vaterunser (dahs FAH-ter-oon-ser)

Vater (FAH-ter) **unser** (OON-ser),

der (dehr) **du** (doo) **bist** (bist) **im** (im) **Himmel** (HIM-mel),

geheiligt (guh-HY-licht) **werde** (VEHR-duh) **dein** (dine) **Name** (NAH-meh).

Dein (dine) **Reich** (rykh — like "rye" + harsh German "ch") **komme** (KOH-meh).

Dein (dine) **Wille** (VIL-leh) **geschehe** (guh-SHAY-eh),

wie (vee) **im** (im) **Himmel** (HIM-mel) **so** (zo) **auf** (owf) **Erden** (AIR-den).

Unser (OON-ser) **tägliches** (TAY-gli-khes) **Brot** (broht) **gib** (gip) **uns** (oons) **heute** (HOY-tuh).

Und (oont) **vergib** (fehr-GIP) **uns** (oons) **unsere** (OON-zeh-ruh) **Schuld** (shoolt),

wie (vee) **auch** (owkh) **wir** (veer) **vergeben** (fehr-GAY-ben) **unsern** (OON-zern) **Schuldigern** (SHOOL-dih-gairn).

Und (oont) **führe** (FÜH-reh) **uns** (oons) **nicht** (nikht) **in** (in) **Versuchung** (fehr-ZOO-khoong),

sondern (ZON-dern) **erlöse** (air-LÖH-zeh) **uns** (oons) **von** (fon) **dem** (daym) **Bösen** (BÖH-zen).

Amen. (AH-men)

Understanding the German Alphabet

Alphabet
- German uses the Latin alphabet with **26 letters (A–Z)**, plus three additional letters: **Ä, Ö, Ü**, and the ligature **ß**.
- Alphabet order: … X, Y, Z, Ä, Ö, Ü.
- Letters **Q, W, X, Y** are standard; **ß** appears only in lowercase and never at the start of a word.

Letter Sounds Differ from English
- **A** = *ah* (Mann = mahn).
- **Ä** = like *e* in *bed* (Bär = beh-r).
- **E** = can be long *eh* (Seele = zeh-leh) or short *e* (Bett = bet).
- **I** = *ee* (Liebe = lee-beh).
- **O** = *oh* (Brot = broht).
- **Ö** = like French *peur* or rounded "er" sound (schön = shœn).
- **U** = *oo* (gut = goot).
- **Ü** = fronted *ee* with rounded lips, like French *u* (müde = mü-deh).
- **J** = "y" as in *yes* (ja = yah).
- **K** = always hard *k* (Katze = kaht-zeh).
- **G** = hard *g* (gut = goot), soft *g* as in *y* in some dialects before front vowels.
- **H** = pronounced at the start of words, silent after vowels (haben = hah-ben; sehen = zay-en).
- **R** = rolled or uvular, depending on dialect.
- **S** = *z* at the start of words before vowels (Sohn = zohn), *s* elsewhere (Haus = house).
- **ß** = sharp *s* (Straße = shtrah-seh).
- **V** = usually *f* (Vater = fah-ter), sometimes *v* in loanwords.
- **W** = *v* (Wasser = vah-ser).
- **Z** = *ts* (Zug = tsoog).
- **Double consonants** = pronounced longer: *Mitte* (midpoint = mit-teh) vs. *Mite* (mite = mee-teh).

Accent Marks
- **Umlauts (¨)** on **Ä, Ö, Ü** change the vowel sound.
- **Acute or grave accents** are rare; mainly appear in loanwords (café, à la carte).
- Stress usually falls on the **first syllable** but can vary in compound words.

58

Understanding German Grammar

Nouns and Gender
- German has **three genders**: masculine, feminine, neuter.
  - Masculine: *der Mann* = the man.
  - Feminine: *die Frau* = the woman.
  - Neuter: *das Kind* = the child.
- Nouns are always capitalized.
- Plural formation is irregular and varies by gender and ending:
  - *der Mann* → *die Männer* (man → men).
  - *die Frau* → *die Frauen* (woman → women).
  - *das Kind* → *die Kinder* (child → children).

Articles
- **Definite**: *der (m.), die (f.), das (n.), die (pl.).*
- **Indefinite**: *ein (m./n.), eine (f.).*
- Articles must agree in **gender, number, and case**.

Adjectives
- Placed before nouns: *ein rotes Haus* = a red house.
- Must agree in gender, number, and case.
- Strong, weak, or mixed declension depends on whether the noun is preceded by a definite or indefinite article.

Pronouns
- Subject: *ich, du, er, sie, es, wir, ihr, sie, Sie.*
- Object: *mich, dich, ihn, sie, es, uns, euch, sie, Sie.*
- Possessive: *mein, dein, sein, ihr, unser, euer, ihr, Ihr* (declined according to gender, number, and case).
- Reflexive: *mich, dich, sich, uns, euch, sich.*
- German is **not pro-drop**: subject pronouns are required.

Verbs
- Three main conjugation types: weak (regular), strong (irregular), and mixed.
- Key tenses:
  - **Present tense**: *ich spreche* (I speak).
  - **Simple past tense**: *ich sprach* (I spoke).
  - **Present perfect tense**: *ich habe gesprochen* (I have spoken).
  - **Past perfect tense**: *ich hatte gesprochen* (I had spoken).
  - **Future tense**: *ich werde sprechen* (I will speak).
- Modal verbs (*können, müssen, wollen, sollen, dürfen, mögen*) take bare infinitives.

- Subjunctive I and II for indirect speech, wishes, or hypotheticals: *Ich wünschte, ich hätte Zeit* (I wished, I had time).

Word Order

- Standard **SVO** (subject–verb–object): *Maria isst Brot* (Maria eats bread).
- Main clauses: **V2 rule** (*Ich lese ein Buch* = I read a book).
- Subordinate clauses: verb moves to the end: *..., weil ich ein Buch lese* (because I a book am reading).
- Negation: *nicht* (verb/adjective/phrase) or *kein* (noun).

Questions

- Yes/No questions are inverted: *Sprichst du Deutsch?* (Speak you German?).
- Question words: *wer* (who), *was* (what), *wo* (where), *wann* (when), *warum* (why), *wie* (how).

Prepositions

- Govern cases: accusative (*für, durch, gegen, ohne, um*), dative (*aus, bei, mit, nach, seit, von, zu*), genitive (*während, wegen, trotz*).
- Prepositions often determine article endings (*mit dem Mann* = with the man).

Special Features

- Compound nouns are common: *Donaudampfschifffahrtsgesellschaftskapitän* (Danube steam ship travel company captain).
- Articles, adjectives, and pronouns are **declined for case, gender, and number**, making German highly inflected.
- Word endings often indicate gender (e.g., *-ung* = feminine, *-chen* = neuter).

Chapter XI

Icelandic

The Lords Prayer in *Íslenska* (Icelandic)

Faðir vor

Faðir vor, þú sem ert á himnum,
helgist þitt nafn,
tilkomi ríki þitt,
verði þinn vilji,
svo sem á himni, svo á jörðu.
Gef oss í dag vort daglegt brauð,
og fyrirgef oss vorar skuldir,
svo sem vér fyrirgefum vorum skuldunautum,
og eigi leið þú oss í freistingar,
heldur frelsa oss frá illu.
Amen.

Word-to-Word Translation

Faðir vor (The Our Father)

Faðir vor, (Father our,)

þú (you) **sem** (who) **ert** (are) **á** (on) **himnum,** (heaven,)

helgist (be hallowed) **þitt** (your) **nafn,** (name,)

tilkomi (come) **ríki** (kingdom) **þitt,** (your,)

verði (be) **þinn** (your) **vilji,** (will,)

svo (as) **sem** (as) **á** (on) **himni,** (heaven,) **svo** (so) **á** (on) **jörðu.** (earth.)

Gef (Give) **oss** (us) **í** (in) **dag** (day) **vort** (our) **daglegt** (daily) **brauð,** (bread,)

og (and) **fyrirgef** (forgive) **oss** (us) **vorar** (our) **skuldir,** (debts,)

svo (as) **sem** (as) **vér** (we) **fyrirgefum** (forgive) **vorum** (our) **skuldunautum,** (debtors,)

og (and) **eigi** (not) **leið** (lead) **þú** (you) **oss** (us) **í** (into) **freistingar,** (temptation,)

heldur (but) **frelsa** (deliver) **oss** (us) **frá** (from) **illu.** (evil.)

Amen. (Amen.)

Phonetic Pronunciation

Faðir vor (FAH-thir vor)

Faðir (FAH-thir) **vor** (vor),

þú (thoo) **sem** (sem) **ert** (airt) **á** (ow, like *cow*) **himnum** (HIM-noom),

helgist (HEL-gist) **þitt** (thit) **nafn** (nahvn — short "a," *vn* tight),

tilkomi (TIL-koh-mi) **ríki** (REE-ki) **þitt** (thit),

verði (VAIR-thi) **þinn** (thin) **vilji** (VIL-yih),

svo (svoh) **sem** (sem) **á** (ow) **himni,** (HIM-ni) **svo** (svoh) **á** (ow) **jörðu** (YUR-thu — "ö" like German *ö*).

Gef (Gyev — "gy" like soft g) **oss** (oss) **í** (ee) **dag** (dahg) **vort** (vort) **daglegt** (DAHG-lekht) **brauð** (BROY-th — "au" = öy, ð = th in *this*),

og (ohg) **fyrirgef** (FIR-ir-gyef) **oss** (oss) **vorar** (VOH-rar) **skuldir** (SKOOL-dir),

svo (svoh) **sem** (sem) **vér** (vyair — like "v" + *air*) **fyrirgefum** (FIR-ir-gyef-oom) **vorum** (VOH-room) **skuldunautum** (SKOOL-doo-nøy-toom),

og (ohg) **eigi** (AY-yi) **leið** (layth) **þú** (thoo) **oss** (oss) **í** (ee) **freistingar** (FRAY-sting-ar),

heldur (HEL-thur) **frelsa** (FREL-sa) **oss** (oss) **frá** (frow) **illu** (EEL-loo).

Amen. (AH-men)

Understanding the Icelandic Alphabet

Alphabet

- Icelandic has **32 letters**, including the standard Latin 26 (**A–Z**) plus the special letters **Á, Ð, É, F́, Ǵ, Í, Ó, Ö, Þ, Ú, Ý, Æ, Ø** (*note: some appear in modern usage as accented forms*). The core additional letters used in everyday Icelandic are: **Á, Ð, É, Í, Ó, Ö, Þ, Ú, Ý, Æ**.
- Alphabet order: … X, Y, Z, Á, Ð, É, F́, Ǵ, Í, Ó, Ö, Þ, Ú, Ý, Æ.
- Letters **C, Q, W, Z** appear only in loanwords, foreign names, or older texts.

Letter Sounds Differ from English

- **A** = *ah* (maður = ma-thur).
- **Á** = long *au* (sá = sow).
- **Æ** = like *i* in *ice* (bæ = bye).
- **E** = short *eh* (fer = fehr).
- **É** = long *yeh* (sér = syehr).
- **I** = *ee* (hí = hee).
- **Í** = long *ee* (lík = leek).
- **O** = *oh* (sonur = so-nur).
- **Ó** = long *o* (fóður = fo-dur).
- **Ö** = like German *ö* or French *peur* (bön = bœn).
- **U** = *oo* (hundur = hoond-ur).
- **Ú** = long *oo* (rút = root).
- **Y** = fronted *ee* with rounded lips (ýra = ee-ra).
- **Ý** = long version of *Y* (dýr = dee-r).
- **Ð (eth)** = soft *th* as in *this* (við = vith).
- **Þ (thorn)** = hard *th* as in *thing* (þing = thing).
- **J** = "y" as in *yes* (jökull = yohk-ull).
- **G** = hard *g* (góð = goh-th); soft before front vowels like *y* or *i* (gefa = yeh-va).
- **R** = rolled or tapped.
- **V** = like English *v*.
- **F** = *f*; pronounced *v* between vowels (afa = a-va).
- **Double consonants** = pronounced longer: *kolli* (peak) vs. *koli* (coat).

Accent Marks

- Accents indicate **vowel length** (á, é, í, ó, ú, ý, ýr).
- **Eth (Ð)** and **thorn (Þ)** are unique letters, not accents, and affect pronunciation.
- Stress almost always falls on the **first syllable**.

Understanding Icelandic Grammar

Nouns and Gender
- Icelandic has **three genders**: masculine, feminine, neuter.
  - o   Masculine: *maður* = man.
  - o   Feminine: *kona* = woman.
  - o   Neuter: *barn* = child.
- Nouns are **declined for four cases**: nominative, accusative, dative, genitive.
- Plurals are formed irregularly depending on gender and declension class:
  - o   *maður* → *menn* (man → men).
  - o   *kona* → *konur* (woman → women).
  - o   *barn* → *börn* (child → children).

Articles
- Icelandic has **no separate definite article before the noun**. The definite form is **suffixed**:
  - o   Masculine: *hestur* → *hesturinn* (the horse).
  - o   Feminine: *kona* → *konan* (the woman).
  - o   Neuter: *barn* → *barnið* (the child).
- Indefinite: *hestur, kona, barn* = a/an.

Adjectives
- Must **agree with the noun** in gender, number, and case:
  - o   *góður maður* = good man.
  - o   *góð kona* = good woman.
  - o   *gott barn* = good child.
- Plural: *góðir menn, góðar konur, góð börn.*
- Adjectives are declined just like nouns.

Pronouns
- Subject: *ég, þú, hann, hún, það, við, þið, þeir, þær, þau.*
- Object: *mig, þig, hann, hana, það, okkur, ykkur, þá, þær, þau.*
- Reflexive: *sig.*
- Possessive: *minn, mín, mitt* (agree with noun gender, number, case).
- Icelandic is **not pro-drop**: subjects are usually required.

Verbs
- Verbs **conjugate for person, number, tense, mood, and voice.**

- Strong (irregular) and weak (regular) verbs exist.
- Key tenses:
  - **Present tense**: *ég tala* (I speak).
  - **Past tense**: *ég talaði* (I spoke).
  - **Perfect tense**: *ég hef talað* (I have spoken).
  - **Past perfect tense**: *ég hafði talað* (I had spoken).
  - **Future tense**: *ég mun tala* (I will speak).
- Subjunctive is used for wishes, commands, and certain clauses: *Ég vil að hann komi* (I want him to come).

Word Order
- Standard **SVO** (subject-verb-object): *Ég les bók* (I read a book).
- Main clauses: **V2 rule** *Í dag les ég bók* (Today I read a book).
- Subordinate clauses: verb goes to the end (*...þar sem ég les bók*).
- Negation: *ekki* (after the verb or object): *Ég les ekki bók* = I do not read a book.

Questions
- Yes/No questions are inverted: *Lesur þú bók?* (Do you book?).
- Question words: *hver* (who), *hvað* (what), *hvar* (where), *hvenær* (when), *hvers vegna* (why), *hvernig* (how).

Prepositions
- Govern cases: accusative, dative, or genitive.
- Often idiomatic: *á* (on/at), *í* (in), *með* (with), *fyrir* (for), *hjá* (at/by).

Special Features
- Definite articles are suffixed to nouns.
- Extensive use of **cases** affects nouns, pronouns, adjectives, and numerals.
- Strong and weak verb distinctions are essential for correct conjugation.
- Word endings often indicate gender and case.

Chapter XII

Greek

The Lords Prayer in *Ελληνικά* (Greek)

Ο Πατέρας μας

Πάτερ ἡμῶν,

ὁ ἐν τοῖς οὐρανοῖς,

ἁγιασθήτω τὸ ὄνομά σου·

ἐλθέτω ἡ βασιλεία σου·

γενηθήτω τὸ θέλημά σου,

ὡς ἐν οὐρανῷ καὶ ἐπὶ γῆς·

τὸν ἄρτον ἡμῶν τὸν ἐπιούσιον δὸς ἡμῖν σήμερον·

καὶ ἄφες ἡμῖν τὰ ὀφειλήματα ἡμῶν,

ὡς καὶ ἡμεῖς ἀφήκαμεν τοῖς ὀφειλέταις ἡμῶν·

καὶ μὴ εἰσενέγκῃς ἡμᾶς εἰς πειρασμόν,

ἀλλὰ ῥῦσαι ἡμᾶς ἀπὸ τοῦ πονηροῦ.

ἀμήν.

Word-to-Word Translation

Ο Πατέρας μας (The Our Father)

Πάτερ ἡμῶν, (Father our,)

ὁ (the) ἐν (in) τοῖς (the) οὐρανοῖς, (heavens,)

ἁγιασθήτω (be hallowed) τὸ (the) ὄνομά (name) σου· (your;)

ἐλθέτω (come) ἡ (the) βασιλεία (kingdom) σου· (your;)

γενηθήτω (be done) τὸ (the) θέλημά (will) σου, (your,)

ὡς (as) ἐν (in) οὐρανῷ (heaven) καὶ (and) ἐπὶ (on) γῆς· (earth;)

τὸν (the) ἄρτον (bread) ἡμῶν (our) τὸν (the) ἐπιούσιον (daily) δὸς (give) ἡμῖν (us) σήμερον· (today;)

καὶ (and) ἄφες (forgive) ἡμῖν (us) τὰ (the) ὀφειλήματα (debts) ἡμῶν, (our,)

ὡς (as) καὶ (also) ἡμεῖς (we) ἀφήκαμεν (have forgiven) τοῖς (the) ὀφειλέταις (debtors) ἡμῶν· (our;)

καὶ (and) μὴ (not) εἰσενέγκῃς (lead) ἡμᾶς (us) εἰς (into) πειρασμόν, (temptation,)

ἀλλὰ (but) ῥῦσαι (deliver) ἡμᾶς (us) ἀπὸ (from) τοῦ (the) πονηροῦ. (evil.)

ἀμήν. (Amen.)

Phonetic Pronunciation

Ο (o) Πατέρας (pa-TE-ras) μας (mas)

Πάτερ (PAH-ter) ἡμῶν (ee-MON),

ὁ (ho) ἐν (en) τοῖς (tees) οὐρανοῖς (oo-ra-NEES),

ἁγιασθήτω (ah-yee-as-THEE-to) τὸ (to) ὄνομά (O-no-ma) σου· (soo),

ἐλθέτω (el-THE-to) ἡ (ee) βασιλεία (va-see-LEE-a) σου· (soo),

γενηθήτω (ye-nee-THEE-to) τὸ (to) θέλημά (THE-lee-ma) σου (soo),

ὡς (os) ἐν (en) οὐρανῷ (oo-ra-NO) καὶ (keh) ἐπὶ (e-PEE) γῆς· (yees),

τὸν (ton) ἄρτον (AR-ton) ἡμῶν (ee-MON) τὸν (ton) ἐπιούσιον (e-pee-OO-see-on) δὸς (thos) ἡμῖν (ee-MEEN) σήμερον· (SEE-me-ron),

καὶ (keh) ἄφες (A-fes) ἡμῖν (ee-MEEN) τὰ (ta) ὀφειλήματα (o-fi-LEE-ma-ta) ἡμῶν (ee-MON),

ὡς (os) καὶ (keh) ἡμεῖς (ee-MEES) ἀφήκαμεν (a-FEE-ka-men) τοῖς (tees) ὀφειλέταις (o-fi-LE-tes) ἡμῶν· (ee-MON),

καὶ (keh) μὴ (mee) εἰσενέγκῃς (ee-se-NEN-gees) ἡμᾶς (ee-MAS) εἰς (ees) πειρασμόν (pee-ra-SMON),

ἀλλὰ (a-LA) ῥῦσαι (REE-see) ἡμᾶς (ee-MAS) ἀπὸ (a-PO) τοῦ (too) πονηροῦ (po-nee-ROO).

ἀμήν (a-MEEN).

Understanding the Greek Alphabet

Alphabet
- Greek uses its own script with **24 letters,** in order: **A, B, Γ, Δ, E, Z, H, Θ, I, K, Λ, M, N, Ξ, O, Π, P, Σ, T, Y, Φ, X, Ψ, Ω**.
- Greek letters **do not correspond directly** to Latin letters, though some look similar (A = A, B = V/B, etc.).

Letter Sounds Differ from English
- **A / α** = *ah* (μάνα = ma-na).
- **B / β** = *v* (βιβλίο = vee-vlee-o).
- **Γ / γ** = soft *y* before front vowels (γέλιο = yeh-lee-o); guttural *g* elsewhere (γάτα = gah-ta).
- **Δ / δ** = *th* as in *this* (δέντρο = then-dro).
- **E / ε** = short *eh* (μέλι = meh-lee).
- **Z / ζ** = *zd* or *dz* (ζωή = zoh-ee).
- **H / η** = long *ee* (μήλο = mee-lo).
- **Θ / θ** = *th* as in *thing* (θέμα = theh-ma).
- **I / ι** = *ee* (λίμνη = leem-nee).
- **K / κ** = hard *k* (καφές = kah-fes).
- **Λ / λ** = *l* (λάδι = lah-dee).
- **M / μ** = *m* (μήλο = mee-lo).
- **N / ν** = *n* (νύχτα = neekh-ta).
- **Ξ / ξ** = *ks* (ξενοδοχείο = kse-no-do-hee-o).
- **O / o** = *oh* (όνομα = oh-no-ma).
- **Π / π** = *p* (πατέρας = pa-te-ras).
- **P / ϱ** = trilled or tapped *r* (ρόδο = ro-do).
- **Σ / σ, ς** = *s* (σπίτι = spee-tee).
- **T / τ** = *t* (τυρί = tee-ree).
- **Y / υ** = like French *u* or German *ü* (κύμα = ky-ma).
- **Φ / φ** = *f* (φίλος = fee-los).
- **X / χ** = guttural *kh*, like German *Bach* (χαρά = kha-ra).
- **Ψ / ψ** = *ps* (ψάρι = psa-ri).
- **Ω / ω** = long *o* (ώρα = o-ra).

Accent Marks
- Ancient Greek included **diacritics**; Modern Greek uses **tonos (´)** to mark stress on a syllable in words: μάνα (ma-na).
- Historically, Greek used **polytonic accents** (acute, grave, circumflex) to indicate pitch and vowel length; modern Greek uses only the tonos.
- Stress can change meaning: πόλη (city) vs. πολη (not a word).

70

Understanding Greek Grammar

Nouns and Gender
- Greek has **three genders**: masculine, feminine, neuter.
    - Masculine: *ο άντρας* = the man.
    - Feminine: *η γυναίκα* = the woman.
    - Neuter: *το παιδί* = the child.
- Nouns are **declined for four cases**: nominative, genitive, accusative, vocative.
- Plural forms vary by gender:
    - *άντρας → άντρες* (man → men).
    - *γυναίκα → γυναίκες* (woman → women).
    - *παιδί → παιδιά* (child → children).

Articles
- **Definite articles** must agree with gender, number, and case:
    - Masculine: *ο (nom.), του (gen.), τον (acc.).*
    - Feminine: *η, της, την.*
    - Neuter: *το, του, το.*
- **Indefinite articles** exist only in singular: *ένας (m.), μία (f.), ένα (n.).*

Adjectives
- Usually follow the noun (*ένα σπίτι μεγάλο = a big house*), but can precede for emphasis (*μεγάλο σπίτι*).
- Agree with noun in **gender, number, and case**:
    - Masculine singular: μεγάλος.
    - Feminine singular: μεγάλη.
    - Neuter singular: μεγάλο.
- Plural: *μεγάλοι (m.), μεγάλες (f.), μεγάλα (n.).*

Pronouns
- Subject: *εγώ, εσύ, αυτός, αυτή, αυτό, εμείς, εσείς, αυτοί, αυτές, αυτά.*
- Object: *με, σε, τον, την, το, μας, σας, τους, τις, τα.*
- Possessive: *μου, σου, του/της, μας, σας, τους.*
- Reflexive: *αυτός/η/ο ... τον εαυτό του/της/του.*

Verbs
- Conjugate for **person, number, tense, mood, and voice**.
- Moods: indicative, subjunctive, imperative, conditional.
- Key tenses:

- o **Present tense**: *λέω* (I say).
- o **Past imperfect tense**: *έλεγα* (I was saying/used to say).
- o **Simple past tense**: *είπα* (I said).
- o **Future tense**: *θα πω* (I will say).
- Compound tenses use the auxiliary *έχω* (*έχω πει* = I have said).
- Subjunctive expresses wishes, necessity, or purpose: *va έρθει* = that he/she come.

Word Order
- Flexible due to case marking, but **SVO** (subject-verb-object) is standard: *Η Μαρία τρώει ψωμί* (Maria eats bread).
- Pronouns often precede the verb: *Τον βλέπω* = I see him.

Questions and Negation
- Yes/No questions use intonation (rise and fall of your voice when speaking): *Έρχεται;* (Coming?).
- Question words: *τι* (what), *ποιος/ποια/ποιο* (who), *πού* (where), *πότε* (when), *γιατί* (why), *πώς* (how).
- Negation: *δεν* before the verb (*Δεν μιλάω* = I don't speak).

Prepositions
- Common: *σε* (to/at), *από* (from), *με* (with), *για* (for), *πάνω σε* (on).
- Govern the case of the noun or pronoun that follows.

Special Features
- Greek uses **definite articles with nouns in all cases**, unlike English.
- Verbs are highly inflected, showing tense, mood, voice, person, and number.
- Word endings indicate **gender, number, and case**, giving flexibility in word order.

Chapter XIII

Czech

The Lords Prayer in *Čeština* (Czech)

Otče náš

Otče náš,
který jsi na nebesích,
posvěť se jméno tvé,
přijď království tvé,
buď vůle tvá jako v nebi tak i na zemi.
Chléb náš vezdejší dej nám dnes,
a odpusť nám naše viny,
jakož i my odpouštíme našim viníkům,
a neuveď nás v pokušení,
ale zbav nás od zlého.
Amen.

Word-to-Word Translation

Otče náš (The Our Father)

Otče (Father) **náš,** (our,)

který (who) **jsi** (are) **na** (on) **nebesích,** (heavens,)

posvěť (sanctify) **se** (yourself) **jméno** (name) **tvé,** (your,)

přijď (come) **království** (kingdom) **tvé,** (your,)

buď (be) **vůle** (will) **tvá** (your) **jako** (like) **v** (in) **nebi** (heaven) **tak** (also) **i** (on) **na** (the) **zemi.** (earth.)

Chléb (bread) **náš** (our) **vezdejší** (daily) **dej** (give) **nám** (us) **dnes,** (today,)

a (and) **odpusť** (forgive) **nám** (us) **naše** (our) **viny,** (sins,)

jakož (just as) **i** (also) **my** (we) **odpouštíme** (forgive) **našim** (our) **viníkům,** (offenders,)

a (and) **neuveď** (lead not) **nás** (us) **v** (into) **pokušení,** (temptation,)

ale (but) **zbav** (deliver) **nás** (us) **od** (from) **zlého.** (evil.)

Amen. (Amen.)

Phonetic Pronunciation

Otče (OT-cheh) náš (nahsh)

Otče (OT-cheh) náš (nahsh),

který (KTEH-ree) jsi (ysih) na (nah) nebesích (NEH-beh-seekh),

posvěť (POS-vyeht) se (seh) jméno (YMAY-noh) tvé (tveh),

přijď (PRZHIDJ) království (KRAH-lohv-stvee) tvé (tveh),

buď (boot) vůle (VOO-leh) tvá (tva) jako (YAH-ko) v (v) nebi (NEH-bee) tak (tak) i (ee) na (nah) zemi (ZEH-mee).

Chléb (khlehp) náš (nahsh) vezdejší (VEHZ-day-shee) dej (day) nám (nahm) dnes (dnes),

a (ah) odpusť (OHD-poost) nám (nahm) naše (NAH-sheh) viny (VEE-nih),

jakož (YAH-kosh) i (ee) my (mih) odpouštíme (OHD-po-oo-shtee-meh) našim (NAH-shim) viníkům (VIH-neeh-koom),

a (ah) neuveď (NEH-oo-veht) nás (nahs) v (v) pokušení (POH-koo-sheh-nee),

ale (AH-leh) zbav (zbav) nás (nahs) od (oht) zlého (ZLEH-hoh).

Amen. (AH-men)

Understanding the Czech Alphabet

Alphabet

- Czech uses the Latin alphabet with **42 letters**, including **diacritics** that create distinct sounds. Standard letters: **A, B, C, D, E, F, G, H, I, J, K, L, M, N, O, P, Q, R, S, T, U, V, W, X, Y, Z** plus letters with **háček (ˇ)**: **Č, Ď, Ě, Ň, Ř, Š, Ť, Ž**, and vowels with **acute (´)**: **Á, É, Í, Ó, Ú, Ů, Ý**.
- Alphabet order: … X, Y, Z, Á, Č, Ď, É, Ě, Í, Ň, Ó, Ř, Š, Ť, Ú, Ů, Ý, Ž.
- Letters **Q, W, X** are rare, mostly in loanwords and foreign names.

Letter Sounds Differ from English

- **A / Á** = short *ah* (man = man), long *aa* (máma = maa-ma).
- **E / É** = short *eh* (pes = pes), long *ay* (téma = tay-ma).
- **I / Í** = short *ih* (list = list), long *ee* (víno = vee-no).
- **O / Ó** = short *oh* (rok = rok), long *oh* (lód = lohd).
- **U / Ú / Ů** = long *oo* (dům = doom).
- **Y / Ý** = like *i* (syn = sin), Ý = long *ee* (sýkora = see-ko-ra).
- **C** = *ts* (cena = tseh-na).
- **Č** = *ch* as in *church* (čaj = chai).
- **D / Ď** = *d* (dům = doom), soft palatal *dy* (ďábel = dyah-bel).
- **G** = hard *g* (guma = goo-ma).
- **H** = guttural *h* (hory = ho-ree).
- **J** = *y* as in *yes* (jablko = yah-bl-ko).
- **K** = always hard *k* (kluk = kluk).
- **L / Ĺ / Ľ** = light *l* (list = list), palatal variants in some dialects.
- **M, N / Ň** = standard *m*, *n*; Ň = palatal *ny* (ňadra = nyah-dra).
- **P, R, Ř** = *p* (pes), trilled *r* (ruka), unique rolled-palatal *ř* (řeka ≈ rzh-eh-ka).
- **S / Š** = *s* (sestra), *sh* (škol = shkol).
- **T / Ť** = *t* (tanec), palatal *ty* (ťuk = tyuk).
- **V** = like English *v* (voda).
- **Z / Ž** = *z* (zima), *zh* (žába = zha-ba).
- **Double consonants** = generally pronounced the same as single, lengthening is minimal.

Accent Marks

- **Acute (´)** on vowels marks length: á, é, í, ó, ú, ý.
- **Háček (ˇ)** on consonants changes pronunciation: č, š, ž, ň, ř, ď, ť.
- **Ů** represents a historical long *o* sound, pronounced *oo* today.
- Stress is almost always **on the first syllable**.

Understanding Czech Grammar

Nouns and Gender
- Czech has **three genders**: masculine, feminine, neuter.
    - Masculine animate: *muž* = man.
    - Masculine inanimate: *stůl* = table.
    - Feminine: *žena* = woman.
    - Neuter: *dítě* = child.
- Nouns are **declined for seven cases**: nominative, genitive, dative, accusative, vocative, locative, instrumental.
- Plurals are formed irregularly depending on gender and declension pattern:
    - *muž* → *muži* (man → men).
    - *žena* → *ženy* (woman → women).
    - *dítě* → *děti* (child → children).

Articles
- Czech **does not use definite or indefinite articles**; context determines specificity.

Adjectives
- Must agree with noun in **gender, number, and case**:
    - *nový muž* = new man.
    - *nová žena* = new woman.
    - *nové dítě* = new child.
- Adjective endings change according to the case of the noun.

Pronouns
- Subject: *já, ty, on, ona, ono, my, vy, oni, ony, ona.*
- Object: *mě, tě, ho, ji, je, nás, vás, je.*
- Possessive: *můj, tvůj, jeho, její, náš, váš, jejich* (declined like adjectives).
- Reflexive: *se, si.*
- Czech is **not pro-drop**: subject pronouns are usually included, though they can sometimes be omitted if context is clear.

Verbs
- Conjugate for **person, number, tense, mood, and aspect**.
- Two aspects: imperfective (ongoing/repeated) and perfective (completed).
- Key tenses:

- o **Present tense**: *já mluvím* (I speak).
- o **Past tense**: *já jsem mluvil/mluvila* (I spoke).
- o **Future tense**: imperfective: *já budu mluvit* (I will be speaking), perfective: *já promluvím* (I will speak).
- Moods: indicative, conditional, imperative.
- Reflexive verbs use *se* or *si*: *umýt se* (to wash oneself).

Word Order

- Generally, **SVO** (subject-verb-object): *Petr čte knihu* (Peter reads a book).
- Word order is flexible due to case marking and is used to indicate emphasis.

Questions and Negation

- Yes/No questions use intonation: *Mluvíš česky?* (You speak Czech?).
- Question words: *kdo* (who), *co* (what), *kde* (where), *kdy* (when), *proč* (why), *jak* (how).
- Negation: *ne* before the verb (*Nepíšu* = I do not write).

Prepositions

- Govern cases: accusative, dative, genitive, locative, instrumental.
- Common: *do* (to/into), *z* (from), *s/sa* (with), *na* (on/at), *pro* (for).

Special Features

- Czech is highly inflected; endings indicate **case, number, and gender**, giving flexibility in word order.
- Aspect is essential for expressing completed vs. ongoing actions.
- No articles, so context and word endings determine definiteness.

Chapter XIV

Slovak

The Lords Prayer in *Slovenčina.* (Slovak)

Otče náš

Otče náš,
ktorý si na nebesiach,
posväť sa meno tvoje,
príď kráľovstvo tvoje,
buď vôľa tvoja ako v nebi, tak i na zemi.
Chlieb náš každodenný daj nám dnes,
a odpusť nám naše viny,
ako i my odpúšťame našim vinníkom,
a neuveď nás do pokušenia,
ale zbav nás od zlého.
Amen.

Word-to-Word Translation

Otče náš (The Our Father)

Otče (Father) náš, (our,)

ktorý (who) si (are) na (on) nebesiach, (heavens,)

posvät' (sanctify) sa (yourself) meno (name) tvoje, (your,)

príď (come) kráľovstvo (kingdom) tvoje, (your,)

buď (be) vôľa (will) tvoja (your) ako (as) v (in) nebi, (heaven,)

tak (so) i (also) na (on) zemi. (earth.)

Chlieb (bread) náš (our) každodenný (daily) daj (give) nám (us) dnes, (today,)

a (and) odpust' (forgive) nám (us) naše (our) viny, (sins,)

ako (as) i (also) my (we) odpúšťame (forgive) našim (our) vinníkom, (offenders,)

a (and) neuveď (do not lead) nás (us) do (into) pokušenia, (temptation,)

ale (but) zbav (deliver) nás (us) od (from) zlého. (evil.)

Amen. (Amen.)

Phonetic Pronunciation

Otče (OHT-cheh) **náš** (nahsh),

Otče (OHT-cheh) **náš** (nahsh),

ktorý (KTOH-ree) **si** (see) **na** (nah) **nebesiach,** (NEH-beh-syahkh) **posvät'** (POHS-vyat') **sa** (sah) **meno** (MEH-noh) **tvoje** (TVOH-yeh),

príd' (pree-dj) **kráľovstvo** (KRAA-lyohv-stvoh) **tvoje** (TVOH-yeh),

buď (boot) **vôľa** (VWOH-lya) **tvoja** (TVOH-ya) **ako** (AH-koh) **v** (v) **nebi** (NEH-bee),

tak (tahk) **i** (ee) **na** (nah) **zemi** (ZEH-mee).

Chlieb (khlyehp) **náš** (nahsh) **každodenný** (KAHZH-do-den-nee) **daj** (dai) **nám** (nahm) **dnes** (dnes),

a (ah) **odpust'** (OHD-poost') **nám** (nahm) **naše** (NAH-sheh) **viny** (VEE-nee),

ako (AH-koh) **i** (ee) **my** (mih) **odpúšťame** (OHD-poo-shtyah-meh) **našim** (NAH-shim) **vinníkom** (VEEN-nee-kohm),

a (ah) **neuveď** (NEH-oo-veht') **nás** (nahs) **do** (doh) **pokušenia** (POH-koo-sheh-nyah),

ale (AH-leh) **zbav** (zbav) **nás** (nahs) **od** (oht) **zlého** (ZLEH-hoh).

Amen. (AH-men)

<u>Understanding the Slovak Alphabet</u>

Alphabet

- Slovak uses the Latin alphabet with **46 letters**, including letters with diacritics: **á, č, ď, é, í, Í, ľ, ň, ó, ô, ŕ, š, ť, ú, ý, ž.**
- Standard Latin letters: **A–Z,** plus the letters with diacritics listed above.
- Alphabet order: … X, Y, Z, Á, Č, Ď, É, Í, Ĺ, Ľ, Ň, Ó, Ô, Ŕ, Š, Ť, Ú, Ý, Ž.
- Letters **Q, W** appear mainly in loanwords and foreign names.

Letter Sounds Differ from English

- **A / Á** = short *ah* (man = man), long *aa* (mám = maam).
- **E / É** = short *eh* (ten = ten), long *ay* (téma = tay-ma).
- **I / Í** = short *ih* (list = list), long *ee* (víno = vee-no).
- **O / Ó / Ô** = short *oh* (dom = dom), long *oh* (dóm = dohm), ô = diphthong *uo* (kôň ≈ k-uo-n).
- **U / Ú** = *oo* (muž = moozh).
- **Y / Ý** = like *i* (syn = sin), long *ee* (sýty = see-tee).
- **C** = *ts* (cesta = tseh-sta).
- **Č** = *ch* as in *church* (čaj = chai).
- **D / Ď** = *d* (dom = dom), palatal *dy* (ďakujem = dyah-koo-yem).
- **G** = hard *g* (guma = goo-ma).
- **H** = guttural *h* (hora = ho-ra).
- **J** = *y* as in *yes* (jablko = yah-bl-ko).
- **K** = hard *k* (kluk = kluk).
- **L / Ĺ / Ľ** = light *l* (list = list), palatal variants in some contexts.
- **M, N / Ň** = standard *m, n*; Ň = palatal *ny* (ňadro = nyah-dro).
- **P, R / Ŕ** = *p* (pes), trilled *r* (ryba), Ŕ = long trilled *r* in some contexts.
- **S / Š** = *s* (sestra), *sh* (škol = shkol).
- **T / Ť** = *t* (tanec), palatal *ty* (ťuk = tyuk).
- **V** = like English *v* (voda).
- **Z / Ž** = *z* (zima), *zh* (žaba = zha-ba).
- **R / Ŕ** = rolled or trilled; can appear long in some words.
- **Double consonants** = generally pronounced the same as single; lengthening is minor.

Accent Marks

- **Acute** (´) on vowels indicates long vowels: á, é, í, ó, ú, ý.
- **Háček** (ˇ) on consonants changes pronunciation: č, ď, ľ, ň, š, ť, ž.
- **Ô** represents a diphthong /uo/.
- Stress is **almost always on the first syllable** of words.

Understanding Slovak Grammar

Nouns and Gender
- Slovak has **three genders**: masculine, feminine, neuter.
  - Masculine animate: *muž* = man.
  - Masculine inanimate: *stôl* = table.
  - Feminine: *žena* = woman.
  - Neuter: *dieťa* = child.
- Nouns are **declined for seven cases**: nominative, genitive, dative, accusative, vocative, locative, instrumental.
- Plurals vary by gender and declension pattern:
  - *muž* → *muži* (man → men).
  - *žena* → *ženy* (woman → women).
  - *dieťa* → *deti* (child → children).

Articles
- Slovak **does not use definite or indefinite articles**; context indicates definiteness.

Adjectives
- Agree with noun in **gender, number, and case**:
  - *nový muž* = new man.
  - *nová žena* = new woman.
  - *nové dieťa* = new child.
- Adjective endings change according to the case of the noun.

Pronouns
- Subject: *ja, ty, on, ona, ono, my, vy, oni, ony, ona.*
- Object: *ma, ťa, ho, ju, ho, nás, vás, ich.*
- Possessive: *môj, tvoj, jeho, jej, náš, váš, ich* (declined like adjectives).
- Reflexive: *sa, si.*
- Slovak is **not pro-drop**, though subject pronouns can be omitted if context is clear.

Verbs
- Conjugate for **person, number, tense, mood, and aspect**.
- Two aspects: imperfective (ongoing/repeated) and perfective (completed).
- Key tenses:
  - **Present tense**: *ja hovorím* (I speak).

- o **Past tense**: *ja som hovoril/ hovorila* (I spoke).
- o **Future tense**: imperfective: *ja budem hovoriť* (I will be speaking), perfective: *ja poviem* (I will speak).
- Moods: indicative, conditional, imperative.
- Reflexive verbs use *sa* or *si*: *umyť sa* = to wash oneself.

Word Order
- Generally, **SVO** (subject-verb-object): *Peter číta knihu* (Peter reads a book).
- Flexible due to case endings; word order emphasizes focus or contrast.

Questions and Negation
- Yes/No questions use intonation: *Hovoríš po slovensky?* (You speak in Slovak?).
- Question words: *kto* (who), *čo* (what), *kde* (where), *kedy* (when), *prečo* (why), *ako* (how).
- Negation: *ne* before the verb (*Nehovorím* = I do not speak).

Prepositions
- Govern cases: accusative, dative, genitive, locative, instrumental.
- Common: *do* (to/into), *z* (from), *s/so* (with), *na* (on/at), *pre* (for).

Special Features
- Slovak is highly inflected; endings indicate **case, number, and gender**, allowing flexible word order.
- Verb aspect is crucial for expressing completed vs. ongoing actions.
- No articles: context and word endings determine definiteness.

Chapter XV

Irish

<u>**The Lords Prayer in *Gaeilge*. (Irish)**</u>

Ár nAthair

Ár nAthair atá ar neamh,
go naofar d'ainm,
go dtaga do ríocht,
go ndéantar do thoil ar an talamh,
mar a dhéantar ar neamh.
Ár n-arán laethúil tabhair dúinn inniu,
agus maith dúinn ár bhfiacha,
mar a mhaithimidne dár bhféichiúna féin.
Agus ná lig sinn i gcathú,
ach saor sinn ó olc.
Amen.

Word-to-Word Translation

An tAthair Ár (The Our Father)

Ár (Our) nAthair (Father) atá (who is) ar (on) neamh, (heaven,)

go (that) naofar (be sanctified) d'ainm, (your name,)

go (that) dtaga (come) do (your) ríocht, (kingdom,)

go (that) ndéantar (be done) do (your) thoil (will) ar (on) an (the) talamh, (earth,)

mar (as) a (that) dhéantar (is done) ar (on) neamh. (heaven.)

Ár (Our) n-arán (bread) laethúil (daily) tabhair (give) dúinn (us) inniu, (today,)

agus (and) maith (forgive) dúinn (us) ár (our) bfiacha, (debts,)

mar (as) a (that) mhaithimidne (we forgive) dár (our) bféichiúna (debtors) féin. (ourselves.)

Agus (and) ná (not) lig (let) sinn (us) i (into) gcathú, (temptation,)

ach (but) saor (deliver) sinn (us) ó (from) olc. (evil.)

Amen. (Amen.)

Phonetic Pronunciation

An (un) tAthair (TAH-hir) Ár (awr)

Ár (awr) nAthair (NAH-hir) atá (uh-TAW) ar (er) neamh (nyav),

go (guh) naofar (NEE-fur) d'ainm (DAHN-im),

go (guh) dtaga (DAH-guh) do (duh) ríocht (REE-ukht),

go (guh) ndéantar (NYAYN-tur) do (duh) thoil (HIL) ar (er) an (un) talamh (TAH-luhv),

mar (mahr) a (uh) dhéantar (YAYN-tur) ar (er) neamh (nyav).

Ár (awr) n-arán (nah-RAHN) laethúil (LAH-hoo-il) tabhair (TOOR) dúinn (doo-in) inniu (IN-yoo),

agus (AH-gus) maith (wah) dúinn (doo-in) ár (awr) bfiacha (BEE-uh-khah),

mar (mahr) a (uh) mhaithimidne (WAH-him-id-nyeh) dár (dawr) bféichiúna (BAY-hyoo-na) féin (fayn).

Agus (AH-gus) ná (naw) lig (lig) sinn (shin) i (ee) gcathú (GAH-hoo),

ach (ahkh) saor (seer) sinn (shin) ó (oh) olc (ulk).

Amen (AH-men).

Understanding the Irish Alphabet

Alphabet
- Modern Irish uses the **Latin alphabet** with **18 letters: A, B, C, D, E, F, G, H, I, L, M, N, O, P, R, S, T, U.**
- Letters **J, K, Q, V, W, X, Y, Z** appear only in loanwords, foreign names, or modern borrowings.
- Alphabet order: … O, P, R, S, T, U.
- Irish orthography uses **acute accents (fada)** on vowels to indicate length: **Á, É, Í, Ó, Ú.**

Letter Sounds Differ from English
- **A / Á** = short *ah* (madra = ma-dra), long *aa* (bád = baad).
- **B** = *b* as in English (bád = baad).
- **C** = always hard *k* (cat = kat).
- **D** = *d*, sometimes slender *dy* before i or e (déan = dyane).
- **E / É** = short *eh* (ceann = kyahn), long *ay* (béal = bay-al).
- **F** = *f* (focal = fo-kal).
- **G** = hard *g* (gasúr = ga-soor); softens to *gy* before e or i.
- **H** = used after a consonant to indicate lenition (b → bh, c → ch).
- **I / Í** = short *ih* (ionad = in-ad), long *ee* (míní = mee-nee).
- **L** = *l*; slender before i or e, broad before a, o, u.
- **M** = *m*; slender before i or e, broad before a, o, u.
- **N / Ń** = *n*; slender *ny* before i or e.
- **O / Ó** = short *o* (son = sun), long *oh* (bó = boh).
- **P** = *p*; lenited as *ph* = *f*.
- **R** = trilled or tapped (rós = ros).
- **S / Sh** = *s*; lenited as *sh* = *h* or soft *s*.
- **T** = *t*; slender *ty* before i or e.
- **U / Ú** = short *oo* (tus = toos), long *oo* (lú = loo).

Accent Marks
- **Fada (´)** marks long vowels: Á, É, Í, Ó, Ú.
- Lenition (h added after consonant) changes pronunciation and sometimes meaning: *bád* (boat) vs. *bhád* (not standard, but shows softened b).
- Stress generally falls on the **first syllable**.

Understanding Irish Grammar

Nouns and Gender
- Irish has **two genders**: masculine and feminine.
  - Masculine: *an fear* = the man.
  - Feminine: *an bhean* = the woman.
- Gender affects **mutations** (changes at the start of words):
  - Lenition (softening, e.g., *bean* → *bhean*).
  - Eclipsis (prefixing, e.g., *bád* → *mbád* in some contexts).
- Nouns are **declined for number** (singular/plural) and **case** (nominative, genitive, vocative).

Articles
- Definite article: *an* (singular), *na* (plural).
- No indefinite article; *a* (one) can be used: *fear* = man, *duine* = a person.

Adjectives
- Usually **follow the noun**: *teach mór* = big house.
- Agree in number and case, not strictly in gender.
- Mutations can affect adjectives after certain prepositions or possessives.

Pronouns
- Subject: *mé* = I, *tú* = you, *sé* = he, *sí* = she, *muid/sinn* = we, *sibh* = you(pl), *siad* = they.
- Object: *mé* = me, *thú* = you, *é* = him, *í* = her, *sinn* = us, *sibh* = you(pl), *iad* = them.
- Possessive pronouns trigger **mutations** on nouns: *mo* = my, *do* = your, *a* = his/her, *ár* = our, *bhur* = your(pl), *a* = their.

Verbs
- Conjugated for **person, number, tense, mood, and aspect**.
- Two main forms: **independent** (used in statements) and **dependent** (after particles like *ní* = not, *an* = question).
- Key tenses:
  - **Present tense**: *tá mé* (I am).
  - **Past tense**: *bhí mé* (I was).
  - **Future tense**: *beidh mé* (I will be).

- Irregular verbs are common (e.g., *bí* = to be, *téigh* = to go, *feic* = to see).

Word Order
- Standard **VSO** (verb–subject–object) in independent clauses: *Itheann Sé úll* (He eats an apple).
- Object pronouns often follow the verb in short forms.

Questions and Negation
- Yes/No questions: particle *an* + verb (*An itheann sé úll?* = Does he eat an apple?).
- Negation: *ní* + verb (*Ní itheann sé úll* = He does not eat an apple).
- Question words: *cé* = who, *cad* = what, *cá* = where, *cathain* = when, *cén fáth* = why, *conas* = how.

Prepositions
- Often cause **mutations** on following nouns:
  - *ar an mbord* = on the table.
  - *le mo chara* = with my friend.
- Common prepositions: *ar* = on/at, *i* = in, *le* = with, *do* = to/for, *ó* = from.

Special Features
- Irish is **VSO**, unlike most European languages.
- Mutations are a key feature, affecting the initial consonant of nouns, adjectives, and sometimes verbs.
- No articles for indefinite nouns; definite article triggers case and sometimes mutations.

Chapter XVI

Polish

<u>**The Lords Prayer in *Polski*. (Polish)**</u>

Ojcze Nasz

Ojcze nasz,
któryś jest w niebie,
święć się imię Twoje,
przyjdź królestwo Twoje,
bądź wola Twoja,
jako w niebie, tak i na ziemi.
Chleba naszego powszedniego daj nam dzisiaj,
i odpuść nam nasze winy,
jako i my odpuszczamy naszym winowajcom,
i nie wódź nas na pokuszenie,
ale nas zbaw od złego.
Amen.

<u>Word-to-Word Translation</u>

Ojcze Nasz (The Our Father)

Ojcze (Father) **nasz,** (our,)

któryś (who are) **jest** (is) **w** (in) **niebie,** (heaven,)

święć (sanctify) **się** (yourself) **imię** (name) **Twoje,** (your,)

przyjdź (come) **królestwo** (kingdom) **Twoje,** (your,)

bądź (be) **wola** (will) **Twoja,** (your,)

jako (as) **w** (in) **niebie** (heaven),

tak (so) **i** (also) **na** (on) **ziemi.** (earth.)

Chleba (bread) **naszego** (our) **powszedniego** (daily) **daj** (give) **nam** (us) **dzisiaj,** (today,)

i (and) **odpuść** (forgive) **nam** (us) **nasze** (our) **winy,** (sins,)

jako (as) **i** (also) **my** (we) **odpuszczamy** (forgive) **naszym** (our) **winowajcom,** (offenders,)

i (and) **nie** (not) **wódź** (lead) **nas** (us) **na** (into) **pokuszenie,** (temptation,)

ale (but) **nas** (us) **zbaw** (deliver) **od** (from) **złego.** (evil.)

Amen. (Amen.)

Phonetic Pronunciation

Ojcze (OY-cheh) Nasz (nash)

Ojcze (OY-cheh) nasz (nash),

któryś (KTOO-rish) jest (yest) w (v) niebie (NYEH-byeh),

święć (shfyentsch) się (shyeh) imię (EE-my-eh) Twoje (TVOH-yeh),

przyjdź (PSHIDJ) królestwo (KROO-les-tvoh) Twoje (TVOH-yeh),

bądź (BONDZH) wola (VOH-lah) Twoja (TVOH-yah),

jako (YAH-koh) w (v) niebie (NYEH-byeh),

tak (tahk) i (ee) na (nah) ziemi (ZHYEH-mee),

Chleba (HLEH-bah) naszego (NAH-sheh-goh) powszedniego (POH-fsh-ED-nyeh-goh) daj (dyeh) nam (nahm) dzisiaj (JEE-shy),

i (ee) odpuść (OD-pooshch) nam (nahm) nasze (NAH-sheh) winy (VEE-nih),

jako (YAH-koh) i (ee) my (mih) odpuszczamy (od-POOSH-chah-mee) naszym (NAH-shim) winowajcom (vee-noh-VAI-tsom),

i (ee) nie (nyeh) wódź (voodzh) nas (nahs) na (nah) pokuszenie (poh-KOOSH-neh-nyeh),

ale (AH-leh) nas (nahs) zbaw (zbav) od (od) złego (ZWEH-goh).

Amen (AH-men).

Understanding the Polish Alphabet

Alphabet

- Polish uses the **Latin alphabet** with **32 letters**, including letters with diacritics:
  A, Ą, B, C, Ć, D, E, Ę, F, G, H, I, J, K, L, Ł, M, N, Ń, O, Ó, P, R, S, Ś, T, U, W, Y, Z, Ź, Ż.
- Alphabet order: ... X, Y, Z, Ą, Ć, Ę, Ł, Ń, Ó, Ś, Ź, Ż.
- Letters **Q, V, X** appear mainly in loanwords and foreign names.

Letter Sounds Differ from English

- **A / Ą** = short *ah* (dom = dom), Ą nasalized *on* (ręka ≈ ren-ka).
- **E / Ę** = short *eh* (ten = ten), Ę nasalized *en* (zęby ≈ zen-by).
- **I** = *ee* (lis = lees).
- **O / Ó** = short *oh* (dom = dom), Ó = long *oo* (miód = m-yo-od).
- **U** = *oo* (but = boot).
- **C / Ć** = *ts* (cena = tseh-na), Ć = soft *tsh* (ćma ≈ tch-ma).
- **CZ** = *ch* as in church (czapka = chahp-ka).
- **D / DŹ / DŻ** = d, palatal *dy* (dzień ≈ dye-ny), *j* as in jump (dżem ≈ j-em).
- **G / H / CH** = hard *g*, *h* guttural (góra = goo-ra; horyzont = ho-ri-zont).
- **J** = *y* as in yes (ja = yah).
- **K** = hard *k* (kot = kot).
- **L / Ł** = *l* (light), Ł = *w* (Łódź ≈ woodj).
- **M / N / Ń** = *m*, *n*; Ń = palatal *ny* (koń = k-ohn).
- **R** = trilled or tapped.
- **S / Ś / SZ** = *s* (sesja = ses-ya), Ś = soft *sh* (śpi = shpee), SZ = *sh* (szkoła ≈ shko-wa).
- **T / Ť / CZ / DŹ** = *t*, soft palatal or affricate sounds as above.
- **W** = pronounced like English *v* (woda = vo-da).
- **Z / Ź / Ż** = *z*, soft *zh* (źródło ≈ zh-rood-wo), Ż = *zh* (żaba ≈ zha-ba).
- **Double consonants** = generally pronounced the same; lengthening is minor.

Accent Marks

- **Acute (´)** on consonants (Ć, Ń, Ś, Ź) indicates palatalization.
- **Ogonek (˛)** on vowels (Ą, Ę) indicates nasalization.
- **Ó** = historical long *o* sound, pronounced like *u*.
- Stress is generally **penultimate syllable**, with exceptions in loanwords.

Understanding Polish Grammar

Nouns and Gender
- Polish has **three genders**: masculine, feminine, neuter.
    - Masculine animate: *mężczyzna* = man.
    - Masculine inanimate: *stół* = table.
    - Feminine: *kobieta* = woman.
    - Neuter: *dziecko* = child.
- Nouns are **declined for seven cases**: nominative, genitive, dative, accusative, instrumental, locative, vocative.
- Plural endings vary by gender and declension pattern:
    - *mężczyzna* → *mężczyźni* (man → men).
    - *kobieta* → *kobiety* (woman → women).
    - *dziecko* → *dzieci* (child → children).

Articles
- Polish **does not use definite or indefinite articles**; context conveys specificity.

Adjectives
- Must agree with noun in **gender, number, and case**:
    - *nowy mężczyzna* = new man.
    - *nowa kobieta* = new woman.
    - *nowe dziecko* = new child.
- Adjective endings follow the declension pattern of the noun.

Pronouns
- Subject: *ja, ty, on, ona, ono, my, wy, oni, one.*
- Object: *mnie, cię, go, ją, nas, was, ich.*
- Possessive: *mój, twój, jego, jej, nasz, wasz, ich* (declined like adjectives).
- Reflexive: *się.*
- Polish is **not pro-drop**, though subject pronouns can be omitted if context is clear.

Verbs
- Conjugate for **person, number, tense, aspect, and mood**.
- Two aspects: imperfective (ongoing/repeated) and perfective (completed).
- Key tenses:
    - **Present tense**: *ja mówię* (I speak).

- Past tense: *ja mówiłem/mówiłam* (I spoke).
- Future tense: imperfective: *ja będę mówić* (I will be speaking), perfective: *ja powiem* (I will speak).
- Moods: indicative, conditional, imperative.
- Reflexive verbs use *się*: *myć się* = to wash oneself.

Word Order

- Standard **SVO** (subject-verb-object): *Piotr czyta książkę* (Peter reads a book).
- Word order is flexible due to case markings; used for emphasis or focus.

Questions and Negation

- Yes/No questions use intonation: *Mówisz po polsku?* (You speak in Polish?).
- Question words: *kto* (who), *co* (what), *gdzie* (where), *kiedy* (when), *dlaczego* (why), *jak* (how).
- Negation: *nie* before the verb (*Nie mówię* = I do not speak).

Prepositions

- Govern specific cases (accusative, genitive, dative, instrumental, locative).
- Common: *do* (to), *z/ze* (from), *z* (with), *na* (on/at), *dla* (for).

Special Features

- Polish is highly inflected; endings indicate **case, number, and gender**, giving flexible word order.
- Verb aspect is essential for expressing completed vs. ongoing actions.
- No articles; definiteness is understood from context or demonstratives.

Chapter XVII

Serbian

The Lords Prayer in *Srpski*. (Serbian)

Oče naš

Oče naš,
koji si na nebesima,
sveti se ime tvoje,
dođi carstvo tvoje,
budi volja tvoja,
kao na nebu, tako i na zemlji.
Hleb naš nasušni daj nam danas,
i oprosti nam dugove naše,
kao što i mi opraštamo dužnicima svojim,
i ne uvedi nas u iskušenje,
no izbavi nas od zloga.
Amen.

Word-to-Word Translation

Oče naš (The Our Father)

Oče (Father) naš, (our,)

koji (who) si (are) na (on) nebesima, (heavens,)

sveti (be holy) se (yourself) ime (name) tvoje, (your,)

dođi (come) carstvo (kingdom) tvoje, (your,)

budi (be) volja (will) tvoja, (your,)

kao (as) na (on) nebu (heaven),

tako (so) i (and) na (on) zemlji. (earth.)

Hleb (bread) naš (our) nasušni (daily/necessary) daj (give) nam
(us) danas, (today,)

i (and) oprosti (forgive) nam (us) dugove (debts) naše, (our,)

kao (as) što (that) i (also) mi (we) opraštamo (forgive) dužnicima
(debtors) svojim, (our,)

i (and) ne (not) uvedi (lead) nas (us) u (into) iskušenje,
(temptation,)

no (but) izbavi (deliver) nas (us) od (from) zloga. (evil.)

Amen. (Amen.)

Phonetic Pronunciation

Oče (OH-cheh) naš (nahsh)

Oče (OH-cheh) naš (nahsh),

koji (KOH-yee) si (see) na (nah) nebesima (NEH-beh-see-mah),

sveti (SVEH-tee) se (seh) ime (EE-meh) tvoje (TVOH-yeh),

dođi (DOH-jdee) carstvo (TSAR-stvoh) tvoje (TVOH-yeh),

budi (BOO-dee) volja (VOHL-yah) tvoja (TVOH-yah),

kao (KAH-oh) na (nah) nebu (NEH-boo),

tako (TAH-koh) i (ee) na (nah) zemlji (ZEM-lyee),

Hleb (HLEB) naš (nahsh) nasušni (NAH-soosh-nee) daj (dah-ee)
nam (nahm) danas (DAH-nahs),

i (ee) oprosti (OH-proh-stee) nam (nahm) dugove (DOO-goh-veh)
naše (NAH-sheh),

kao (KAH-oh) što (shtoh) i (ee) mi (mee) opraštamo (OH-prah-
shtah-moh) dužnicima (DOOZH-nee-tseh-moh) svojim (SVOH-
yeem),

i (ee) ne (neh) uvedi (OO-veh-dee) nas (nahs) u (oo) iskušenje
(ees-koo-SHEH-nyeh),

no (noh) izbavi (EES-bah-vee) nas (nahs) od (od) zloga (ZLOH-
gah).

Amen (AH-men).

Understanding the Serbian Alphabet

Alphabet

- Serbian uses **two official alphabets: Cyrillic** and **Latin**, both with **30 letters**.
- **Cyrillic letters**: А, Б, В, Г, Д, Ђ, Е, Ж, З, И, Ј, К, Л, Љ, М, Н, Њ, О, П, Р, С, Т, Ћ, У, Ф, Х, Ц, Ч, Џ, Ш.
- **Latin letters**: A, B, C, Č, Ć, D, Dž, Đ, E, F, G, H, I, J, K, L, Lj, M, N, Nj, O, P, R, S, Š, T, U, V, Z, Ž.
- Both alphabets represent **the same sounds**, so one can switch between them.
- Letters **Q, W, X, Y** appear only in loanwords or foreign names.

Letter Sounds Differ from English

- **A / E / I / O / U** = pure vowels, pronounced as written (baba = bah-bah).
- **Č** = *ch* as in church (čaša = chah-sha).
- **Ć** = softer *ch* (ćerka ≈ tchy-er-ka).
- **Dž** = *j* as in jump (džem = j-em).
- **Đ / Dj** = soft *dj* (đak = dyak).
- **G** = hard *g* (gora = go-ra).
- **H** = like English *h* (hrana = hra-na).
- **J** = *y* as in yes (jelen = yeh-len).
- **K / L / M / N / P / R / S / T / V / Z** = pronounced roughly as in English, with **R** trilled.
- **LJ / NJ** = palatal sounds (ljubav ≈ lyu-bav, njiva ≈ nyi-va).
- **Š / Ž** = *sh* (škola ≈ sh-ko-la), *zh* (žena ≈ zhe-na).
- **C / Č / Ć** = C = *ts* (cvet = ts-vet), Č = *ch*, Ć = soft *ch*.
- **Double consonants** = generally pronounced same as single; lengthening is minor.

Accent Marks

- Standard Serbian does **not use accents** in normal orthography.
- Stress is **dynamic** and usually falls on one of the first syllables of the root; it is **not marked in writing**.
- Loanwords may retain accents or diacritics from other languages.

Understanding Serbian Grammar

Nouns and Gender
- Serbian has **three genders**: masculine, feminine, neuter.
    - Masculine: *muškarac* = man.
    - Feminine: *žena* = woman.
    - Neuter: *dete* = child.
- Nouns are **declined for seven cases**: nominative, genitive, dative, accusative, vocative, instrumental, locative.
- Plural forms vary by gender and declension:
    - *muškarac* → *muškarci* (man → men).
    - *žena* → *žene* (woman → women).
    - *dete* → *deca* (child → children).

Articles
- Serbian **does not use definite or indefinite articles**; context or word order indicates definiteness.

Adjectives
- Agree with nouns in **gender, number, and case**:
    - *novi muškarac* = new man.
    - *nova žena* = new woman.
    - *novo dete* = new child.
- Adjective endings change according to the case of the noun.

Pronouns
- Subject: *ja, ti, on, ona, ono, mi, vi, oni, one, ona.*
- Object: *me, te, ga, je, nas, vas, ih.*
- Possessive: *moj, tvoj, njegov, njen, naš, vaš, njihov* (declined like adjectives).
- Reflexive: *se.*
- Serbian is **not pro-drop**, but subject pronouns can be omitted when context is clear.

Verbs
- Conjugate for **person, number, tense, mood, and aspect**.
- Two aspects: imperfective (ongoing/repeated) and perfective (completed).
- Key tenses:
    - **Present tense**: *ja govorim* (I speak).

- ○ **Past tense**: *ja sam govorio/govorila* (I spoke).
- ○ **Future tense**: imperfective: *ja ću govoriti* (I will be speaking), perfective: *ja ću reći* (I will speak).
- Moods: indicative, imperative, conditional.
- Reflexive verbs use *se*: *prati se* = to wash oneself.

Word Order

- Standard **SVO** (subject-verb-object): *Petar čita knjigu* (Peter reads a book).
- Flexible due to case endings; word order emphasizes focus or contrast.

Questions and Negation

- Yes/No questions use intonation: *Govoriš li srpski?* (You speak Serbian?).
- Question words: *ko* (who), *šta* (what), *gde* (where), *kada* (when), *zašto* (why), *kako* (how).
- Negation: *ne* before the verb (*Ne govorim* = I do not speak).

Prepositions

- Govern specific cases: accusative, genitive, dative, instrumental, locative.
- Common: *u* (in), *na* (on), *sa/s* (with), *do* (to), *od* (from), *za* (for).

Special Features

- Serbian is highly inflected; endings indicate **case, number, and gender**, allowing flexible word order.
- Verb aspect is crucial for expressing completed vs. ongoing actions.
- No articles; definiteness is determined by context or demonstratives.

Chapter XVIII

Bulgarian

The Lords Prayer in *Български* (Bulgarian)

Отче наш

Отче наш,
който си на небесата,
да се свети името Ти,
да дойде царството Ти,
да бъде волята Ти,
както на небето, така и на земята.
Дай ни днес нашия ежедневен хляб,
и прости ни дълговете ни,
както и ние прощаваме на длъжниците си,
и не въведи ни в изкушение,
но избави ни от лукавия.
Амин

Word-to-Word Translation

Отче наш (The Our Father)

Отче (Father) наш, (our,)

който (who) си (are) на (on) небесата, (heavens,)

да (let) се (be) свети (sanctified) името (the name) Ти, (your,)

да (let) дойде (come) царството (the kingdom) Ти, (your,)

да (let) бъде (be) волята (the will) Ти, (your,)

както (as) на (on) небето (heaven),

така (so) и (and) на (on) земята. (earth.)

Дай (Give) ни (us) днес (today) нашия (our) ежедневен (daily) хляб, (bread,)

и (and) прости (forgive) ни (us) дълговете (debts) ни, (our,)

както (as) и (also) ние (we) прощаваме (forgive) на (to) длъжниците (debtors) си, (our,)

и (and) не (not) въведи (lead) ни (us) в (into) изкушение, (temptation,)

но (but) избави (deliver) ни (us) от (from) лукавия. (the evil one.)

Амин. (Amen.)

Phonetic Pronunciation

Отче (OHT-cheh) наш (nahsh)

Отче (OHT-cheh) наш (nahsh),

който (KOY-toh) си (see) на (nah) небесата (neh-beh-SAH-tah),

да (dah) се (seh) свети (SVEH-tee) името (EE-meh-toh) Ти (tee),

да (dah) дойде (DOY-deh) царството (TSAR-stvoh-toh) Ти (tee),

да (dah) бъде (BUE-deh) волята (VOH-lya-tah) Ти (tee),

както (KAHK-toh) на (nah) небето (NEH-beh-toh),

така (TAH-kah) и (ee) на (nah) земята (ZEH-myah-tah),

Дай (DAHY) ни (nee) днес (dness) нашия (NAH-shee-yah) ежедневен (eh-zhdeh-loh-VEHN) хляб (hlyahb),

и (ee) прости (PROH-stee) ни (nee) дълговете (DUL-gohv-teh) ни (nee),

както (KAHK-toh) и (ee) ние (NYEH) прощаваме (proh-SHCHAH-vah-meh) на (nah) длъжниците (DULZH-nee-tseh-teh) си (see),

и (ee) не (neh) въведи (VUH-veh-dee) ни (nee) в (v) изкушение (ees-koo-SHEH-neh),

но (noh) избави (eess-BAH-vee) ни (nee) от (oht) лукавия (loo-KAH-vee-yah).

Амин (AH-meen).

Understanding the Bulgarian Alphabet

Alphabet
- Bulgarian uses the **Cyrillic alphabet** with **30 letters**: А, Б, В, Г, Д, Е, Ж, З, И, Й, К, Л, М, Н, О, П, Р, С, Т, У, Ф, Х, Ц, Ч, Ш, Щ, Ъ, Ь, Ю, Я.
- Letters **Q, W, X, Y** appear only in loanwords or foreign names.
- Bulgarian Cyrillic is **phonemic**, meaning each letter generally represents a single sound.

Letter Sounds Differ from English
- **A, E, I, O, U** = pure vowels, pronounced as written (дом = dom).
- **Ъ** = mid-central vowel, similar to English *u* in *but* (сън = sŭn).
- **Ь** = palatalization marker, softens preceding consonant (място = myasto).
- **Б, В, Г, Д, К, Л, М, Н, П, Р, С, Т, Ф, Х** = pronounced roughly as in English.
- **Ж** = *zh* as in *measure* (жена = zhe-na).
- **Ц** = *ts* (цвят = ts-vyat).
- **Ч** = *ch* as in church (чаша = cha-sha).
- **Ш** = *sh* (школа = shko-la).
- **Щ** = *sht* (ще = shte).
- **Й** = *y* as in yes (йога = yo-ga).
- **Ю** = *yu* (юг = yug).
- **Я** = *ya* (ябълка = ya-bŭl-ka).
- **Double consonants** = generally pronounced the same as single; no length distinction.

Accent Marks
- Bulgarian does **not use accent marks** in standard orthography.
- Stress is **dynamic** and can fall on any syllable; it is **not indicated in writing**.
- Loanwords may retain accents from other languages.

Understanding Bulgarian Grammar

Nouns and Gender
- Bulgarian has **three genders**: masculine, feminine, neuter.
    - *Masculine: мъж (măž)* = man.
    - *Feminine: жена (žena)* = woman.
    - *Neuter: дете (dete)* = child.
- Nouns are **not fully declined** like in other Slavic languages; case is mostly expressed via prepositions.
- Plurals are formed with suffixes:
    - *мъж → мъже* (man → men).
    - *жена → жени* (woman → women).
    - *дете → деца* (child → children).

Articles
- Bulgarian has **postfixed definite articles** (attached to the end of the noun):
    - Masculine: *мъжът* = the man.
    - Feminine: *жената* = the woman.
    - Neuter: *детето* = the child.
- No indefinite article; *един* can be used: *един човек* = a person.

Adjectives
- Agree in **gender and number** with the noun:
    - *нов мъж* = new man.
    - *нова жена* = new woman.
    - *ново дете* = new child.
- Placed **before the noun.**

Pronouns
- Subject: *аз, ти, той, тя, то, ние, вие, те.*
- Object: *мен, те, него, нея, нас, вас, тях.*
- Possessive: *мой, твой, негов, неин, наш, ваш, техен.*
- Reflexive: *се.*
- Bulgarian is **not pro-drop**, but pronouns are often omitted as the verb ending indicates the subject.

Verbs
- Conjugate for **person, number, tense, and mood.**

Bulgarian ~ The Lords Prayer

- Two aspects (imperfective/perfective) are used, especially in past tenses.
- Key tenses:
    - **Present tense**: *аз говоря* (I speak).
    - **Past imperfect tense**: *аз говорех* (I was speaking).
    - **Past aorist tense**: *аз казах* (I spoke).
    - **Future tense**: *аз ще говоря* (I will speak).
- Moods: indicative, imperative, conditional.

Word Order
- Standard **SVO** (subject-verb-object): *Петър чете книга* (Peter reads a book).
- Flexible due to verb endings and context; used for emphasis or contrast.

Questions and Negation
- Yes/No questions use intonation: *Говориш ли български?* (You speak Bulgarian?).
- Question words: *кой* (who), *какво* (what), *къде* (where), *кога* (when), *защо* (why), *как* (how).
- Negation: *не* before the verb (*Не говоря* = I do not speak).

Prepositions
- Govern cases indirectly; case indicated by preposition choice:
    - Common: *в* (in), *на* (on/at), *с* (with), *до* (to), *от* (from), *за* (for).

Special Features
- Bulgarian is **less inflected than other Slavic languages**, with case largely lost.
- Definite articles are **postfixed** rather than separate words.
- Verb aspect is used to distinguish completed vs. ongoing actions.
- Word endings indicate subject and tense, allowing omission of pronouns.

Chapter XIV

Croatian

The Lords Prayer in *Hrvatski* (Croatian)

Oče naš

Oče naš,
koji jesi na nebesima,
sveti se ime tvoje,
dođi kraljevstvo tvoje,
budi volja tvoja,
kako na nebu tako i na zemlji.
Kruh naš svagdanji daj nam danas,
i oprosti nam dugove naše,
kao što i mi opraštamo dužnicima svojim,
i ne uvedi nas u napast,
nego izbavi nas od zla.
Amen.

Word-to-Word Translation

Oče naš (The Our Father)

Oče (Father) **naš,** (our,)

koji (who) **jesi** (are) **na** (on) **nebesima,** (heavens,)

sveti (be holy) **se** (yourself) **ime** (name) **tvoje,** (your,)

dođi (come) **kraljevstvo** (kingdom) **tvoje,** (your,)

budi (be) **volja** (will) **tvoja,** (your,)

kako (as) **na** (on) **nebu** (heaven),

tako (so) **i** (and) **na** (on) **zemlji.** (earth.)

Kruh (bread) **naš** (our) **svagdanji** (daily) **daj** (give) **nam** (us) **danas,** (today,)

i (and) **oprosti** (forgive) **nam** (us) **dugove** (debts) **naše,** (our,)

kao (as) **što** (that) **i** (also) **mi** (we) **opraštamo** (forgive) **dužnicima** (debtors) **svojim,** (our,)

i (and) **ne** (not) **uvedi** (lead) **nas** (us) **u** (into) **napast,** (temptation,)

nego (but/rather) **izbavi** (deliver) **nas** (us) **od** (from) **zla.** (evil.)

Amen. (Amen.)

Phonetic Pronunciation

Oče (OH-cheh) naš (nahsh)

Oče (OH-cheh) naš (nahsh),

koji (KO-yee) jesi (YEH-see) na (nah) nebesima (NEH-beh-see-mah),

sveti (SVEH-tee) se (seh) ime (EE-meh) tvoje (TVOH-yeh),

dođi (DOH-jee) kraljevstvo (KRAH-lyehv-stvoh) tvoje (TVOH-yeh),

budi (BOO-dee) volja (VOHL-yah) tvoja (TVOH-yah),

kako (KAH-koh) na (nah) nebu (NEH-boo),

tako (TAH-koh) i (ee) na (nah) zemlji (ZEM-lyee),

Kruh (KROO) naš (nahsh) svagdanji (SVAHG-dahn-yee) daj (dye) nam (nahm) danas (DAH-nahs),

i (ee) oprosti (OH-proh-stee) nam (nahm) dugove (DOO-goh-veh) naše (NAH-sheh),

kao (KAH-oh) što (SHTOH) i (ee) mi (mee) opraštamo (OH-prahsh-tah-moh) dužnicima (DOOZH-nee-tsee-mah) svojim (SVOH-yeem),

i (ee) ne (neh) uvedi (OO-veh-dee) nas (nahs) u (oo) napast (NAH-pahst),

nego (NEH-goh) izbavi (EEZ-bah-vee) nas (nahs) od (oht) zla (zlah).

Amen (AH-men).

Understanding the Croatian Alphabet

Alphabet

- Croatian uses the **Latin alphabet** with **30 letters**:
  A, B, C, Č, Ć, D, Dž, Đ, E, F, G, H, I, J, K, L, Lj, M, N, Nj, O, P, R, S, Š, T, U, V, Z, Ž.
- Letters **Q, W, X, Y** appear only in loanwords or foreign names.
- Each letter corresponds to a **distinct sound**, making Croatian orthography highly phonetic.

Letter Sounds Differ from English

- **A / E / I / O / U** = pure vowels, pronounced as written (dom = dom).
- **Č** = *ch* as in church (čaj = chah-y).
- **Ć** = softer *ch* (ćerka ≈ tchy-er-ka).
- **Dž** = *j* as in jump (džem = j-em).
- **Đ / Dj** = soft *dj* (đak = dyak).
- **G** = hard *g* (gora = go-ra).
- **H** = like English *h* (hrana = hra-na).
- **J** = *y* as in yes (jabuka = yah-bu-ka).
- **K / L / M / N / P / R / S / T / V / Z** = pronounced roughly as in English, with **R** trilled.
- **LJ / NJ** = palatal sounds (ljubav ≈ lyu-bav, njiva ≈ nyi-va).
- **Š / Ž** = *sh* (škola ≈ sh-ko-la), *zh* (žena ≈ zhe-na).
- **C / Č / Ć** = C = *ts* (cesta = tse-sta), Č = *ch*, Ć = soft *ch*.
- **Double consonants** = generally pronounced the same as single; lengthening is minor.

Accent Marks

- Standard Croatian **does not use accent marks** in spelling.
- Stress is **dynamic** and can fall on any syllable; it is **not indicated in writing**.
- Loanwords may retain accents from other languages.

Understanding Croatian Grammar

Nouns and Gender
- Croatian has **three genders**: masculine, feminine, neuter.
  - o Masculine: *muškarac* = man.
  - o Feminine: *žena* = woman.
  - o Neuter: *dijete* = child.
- Nouns are **declined for seven cases**: nominative, genitive, dative, accusative, vocative, instrumental, locative.
- Plural endings vary by gender and declension:
  - o *muškarac* → *muškarci* (man → men).
  - o *žena* → *žene* (woman → women).
  - o *dijete* → *djeca* (child→ children).

Articles
- Croatian **does not use definite or indefinite articles**; context conveys definiteness.

Adjectives
- Agree with nouns in **gender, number, and case**:
  - o *novi muškarac* = new man.
  - o *nova žena* = new woman.
  - o *novo dijete* = new child.
- Usually placed before the noun.

Pronouns
- Subject: *ja, ti, on, ona, ono, mi, vi, oni, one, ona.*
- Object: *me, te, ga, je, nas, vas, ih.*
- Possessive: *moj, tvoj, njegov, njen, naš, vaš, njihov* (declined like adjectives).
- Reflexive: *se.*
- Croatian is **not pro-drop**, but subject pronouns can be omitted if context is clear.

Verbs
- Conjugate for **person, number, tense, mood, and aspect.**
- Two aspects: imperfective (ongoing/repeated) and perfective (completed).
- Key tenses:
  - o **Present tense**: *ja govorim* (I speak).

- o **Past tense**: *ja sam govorio/govorila (I spoke)*.
- o **Future tense**: imperfective: *ja ću govoriti* (I will be speaking), perfective: *ja ću reći* (I will speak).
- Moods: indicative, imperative, conditional.
- Reflexive verbs use *se*: *prati se* (to wash oneself).

Word Order
- Standard **SVO** (subject-verb-object): *Petar čita knjigu* (Peter reads a book).
- Flexible due to case endings; used for emphasis or contrast.

Questions and Negation
- Yes/No questions use intonation: *Govoriš li hrvatski?* (You speak Croatian?).
- Question words: *tko* (who), *što* (what), *gdje* (where), *kada* (when), *zašto* (why), *kako* (how).
- Negation: *ne* before the verb (*Ne govorim* = I do not speak).

Prepositions
- Govern specific cases (accusative, genitive, dative, instrumental, locative).
- Common: *u* (in), *na* (on), *s/sa* (with), *do* (to), *od* (from), *za* (for).

Special Features
- Croatian is highly inflected; endings indicate **case, number, and gender**, allowing flexible word order.
- Verb aspect is essential for completed vs. ongoing actions.
- No articles; definiteness is understood from context or demonstratives.

Chapter XX

Bosnian

The Lords Prayer in *Bosanski* (Bosnian)

Oče naš

Oče naš,
koji jesi na nebesima,
sveti se ime tvoje,
dođi kraljevstvo tvoje,
budi volja tvoja,
kako na nebu tako i na zemlji.
Kruh naš svagdanji daj nam danas,
i oprosti nam dugove naše,
kao što i mi opraštamo dužnicima svojim,
i ne uvedi nas u napast,
nego izbavi nas od zla.
Amen.

Word-to-Word Translation

Oče naš (The Our Father)

Oče (Father) **naš,** (our,)

koji (who) **jesi** (are) **na** (on) **nebesima,** (heavens,)

sveti (be sanctified) **se** (yourself) **ime** (name) **tvoje,** (your,)

dođi (come) **kraljevstvo** (kingdom) **tvoje,** (your,)

budi (be) **volja** (will) **tvoja,** (your,)

kako (as) **na** (on) **nebu** (heaven) **tako** (so) **i** (and) **na** (on) **zemlji.**
(earth.)

Kruh (bread) **naš** (our) **svagdanji** (daily) **daj** (give) **nam** (us) **danas,**
(today,)

i (and) **oprosti** (forgive) **nam** (us) **dugove** (debts) **naše,** (our,)

kao (as) **što** (that) **i** (also) **mi** (we) **opraštamo** (forgive) **dužnicima**
(debtors) **svojim,** (our,)

i (and) **ne** (not) **uvedi** (lead) **nas** (us) **u** (into) **napast,** (temptation,)

nego (but/rather) **izbavi** (deliver) **nas** (us) **od** (from) **zla.** (evil.)

Amen. (Amen.)

Phonetic Pronunciation

Oče (OH-cheh) **naš** (nahsh)

Oče (OH-cheh) **naš** (nahsh),

koji (KO-yee) **jesi** (YEH-see) **na** (nah) **nebesima** (NEH-beh-see-mah),

sveti (SVEH-tee) **se** (seh) **ime** (EE-meh) **tvoje** (TVOH-yeh),

dođi (DOH-jee) **kraljevstvo** (KRAH-lyehv-stvoh) **tvoje** (TVOH-yeh),

budi (BOO-dee) **volja** (VOHL-yah) **tvoja** (TVOH-yah),

kako (KAH-koh) **na** (nah) **nebu** (NEH-boo),

tako (TAH-koh) **i** (ee) **na** (nah) **zemlji** (ZEM-lyee),

Kruh (KROO) **naš** (nahsh) **svagdanji** (SVAHG-dahn-yee) **daj** (dye) **nam** (nahm) **danas** (DAH-nahs),

i (ee) **oprosti** (OH-proh-stee) **nam** (nahm) **dugove** (DOO-goh-veh) **naše** (NAH-sheh),

kao (KAH-oh) **što** (SHTOH) **i** (ee) **mi** (mee) **opraštamo** (OH-prahsh-tah-moh) **dužnicima** (DOOZH-nee-tsee-mah) **svojim** (SVOH-yeem),

i (ee) **ne** (neh) **uvedi** (OO-veh-dee) **nas** (nahs) **u** (oo) **napast** (NAH-pahst),

nego (NEH-goh) **izbavi** (EEZ-bah-vee) **nas** (nahs) **od** (oht) **zla** (zlah).

Amen (AH-men).

Understanding the Bosnian Alphabet

Alphabet
- Bosnian uses **two alphabets: Latin** and **Cyrillic**, both with **30 letters.**
- **Latin letters:** A, B, C, Č, Ć, D, Dž, Đ, E, F, G, H, I, J, K, L, Lj, M, N, Nj, O, P, R, S, Š, T, U, V, Z, Ž.
- **Cyrillic letters:** А, Б, В, Г, Д, Ђ, Е, Ж, З, И, Ј, К, Л, Љ, М, Н, Њ, О, П, Р, С, Т, Ћ, У, Ф, Х, Ц, Ч, Џ, Ш.
- Letters Q, W, X, Y appear only in foreign words and names.
- Each letter represents a **distinct sound,** making Bosnian highly phonetic.

Letter Sounds Differ from English
- **A / E / I / O / U** = pure vowels, pronounced as written (dom = dom).
- **Č** = *ch* as in church (čaj = chah-y).
- **Ć** = softer *ch* (ćerka ≈ tchy-er-ka).
- **Dž** = *j* as in jump (džem = j-em).
- **Đ / Dj** = soft *dj* (đak = dyak).
- **G** = hard *g* (gora = go-ra).
- **H** = like English *h* (hrana = hra-na).
- **J** = *y* as in yes (jabuka = yah-bu-ka).
- **K / L / M / N / P / R / S / T / V / Z** = pronounced roughly as in English, with **R** trilled.
- **LJ / NJ** = palatal sounds (ljubav ≈ lyu-bav, njiva ≈ nyi-va).
- **Š / Ž** = *sh* (škola ≈ sh-ko-la), *zh* (žena ≈ zhe-na).
- **C / Č / Ć** = C = *ts* (cesta = tse-sta), Č = *ch*, Ć = soft *ch*.
- **Double consonants** = generally pronounced the same as single; lengthening is minor.

Accent Marks
- Standard Bosnian **does not use accent marks** in spelling.
- Stress is **dynamic** and can fall on any syllable; it is **not indicated in writing.**
- Loanwords may retain accents from other languages.

Understanding Bosnian Grammar

Nouns and Gender
- Bosnian has **three genders**: masculine, feminine, neuter.
  - Masculine: *muškarac* = man.
  - Feminine: *žena* = woman.
  - Neuter: *dijete* = child.
- Nouns are **declined for seven cases**: nominative, genitive, dative, accusative, vocative, instrumental, locative.
- Plural endings vary by gender and declension:
  - *muškarac* → *muškarci* (man → men).
  - *žena* → *žene* (woman → women).
  - *dijete* → *djeca* (child → children).

Articles
- Bosnian **does not use definite or indefinite articles**; context conveys definiteness.

Adjectives
- Agree with nouns in **gender, number, and case**:
  - *novi muškarac* = new man.
  - *nova žena* = new woman.
  - *novo dijete* = new child.
- Usually placed **before the noun**.

Pronouns
- Subject: *ja, ti, on, ona, ono, mi, vi, oni, one, ona.*
- Object: *me, te, ga, je, nas, vas, ih.*
- Possessive: *moj, tvoj, njegov, njen, naš, vaš, njihov* (declined like adjectives).
- Reflexive: *se.*
- Bosnian is **not pro-drop**, but subject pronouns can be omitted if context is clear.

Verbs
- Conjugate for **person, number, tense, mood, and aspect**.
- Two aspects: imperfective (ongoing/repeated) and perfective (completed).
- Key tenses:
  - **Present tense**: *ja govorim* (I speak).

- o **Past tense**: *ja sam govorio/govorila* (I spoke).
- o **Future tense**: imperfective: *ja ću govoriti* (I will be speaking), perfective: *ja ću reći* (I will speak).
- Moods: indicative, imperative, conditional.
- Reflexive verbs use *se*: *prati se* (to wash oneself).

Word Order
- Standard **SVO** (subject-verb-object): *Petar čita knjigu* (Peter reads a book).
- Flexible due to case endings; word order emphasizes focus or contrast.

Questions and Negation
- Yes/No questions use intonation: *Govoriš li bosanski?* (You speak Bosnian?).
- Question words: *tko* (who), *šta* (what), *gdje* (where), *kada* (when), *zašto* (why), *kako* (how).
- Negation: *ne* before the verb (*Ne govorim* = I do not speak).

Prepositions
- Govern specific cases (accusative, genitive, dative, instrumental, locative).
- Common: *u* (in), *na* (on), *s/sa* (with), *do* (to), *od* (from), *za* (for).

Special Features
- Bosnian is highly inflected; endings indicate **case, number, and gender**, allowing flexible word order.
- Verb aspect distinguishes completed vs. ongoing actions.
- No articles; definiteness is determined from context or demonstratives.

Chapter XXI

Slovenian

The Lords Prayer in *Slovenščina* (Slovenian)

Oče naš

Oče naš,
ki si v nebesih,
posvečeno bodi tvoje ime.
Pridi tvoje kraljestvo.
Zgodi se tvoja volja,
kakor v nebesih tako tudi na zemlji.
Daj nam danes naš vsakdanji kruh,
in odpusti nam naše dolge,
kakor tudi mi odpuščamo svojim dolžnikom.
In ne vpelji nas v skušnjavo,
temveč reši nas hudega.
Amen.

Word-to-Word Translation

Oče naš (The Our Father)

Oče (Father) naš, (our,)

ki (who) si (are) v (in) nebesih, (heavens,)

posvečeno (hallowed/holy) bodi (be) tvoje (your) ime. (name.)

Pridi (come) tvoje (your) kraljestvo. (kingdom.)

Zgodi se (be done/happen) tvoja (your) volja, (will,)

kakor (as) v (in) nebesih (heavens),

tako (so) tudi (also) na (on) zemlji. (earth.)

Daj (give) nam (us) danes (today) naš (our) vsakdanji (daily) kruh,
(bread,)

in (and) odpusti (forgive) nam (us) naše (our) dolge, (debts,)

kakor (as) tudi (also) mi (we) odpuščamo (forgive) svojim (our)
dolžnikom. (debtors.)

In (and) ne (not) vpelji (lead) nas (us) v (into) skušnjavo,
(temptation,)

temveč (but rather) reši (deliver/save) nas (us) hudega. (evil.)

Amen. (Amen.)

Phonetic Pronunciation

Oče (OH-cheh) **naš** (nahsh)

Oče (OH-cheh) **naš** (nahsh),

ki (kee) **si** (see) **v** (v) **nebesih** (NEH-beh-seekh),

posvečeno (POS-vyeh-cheh-noh) **bodi** (BOH-dee) **tvoje** (TVOH-yeh) **ime** (EE-meh),

Pridi (PREE-dee) **tvoje** (TVOH-yeh) **kraljestvo** (KRAHL-yes-tvoh),

Zgodi (ZGOH-dee) **se** (seh) **tvoja** (TVOH-yah) **volja** (VOHL-yah),

kakor (KAH-kor) **v** (v) **nebesih** (NEH-beh-seekh),

tako (TAH-koh) **tudi** (TOO-dee) **na** (nah) **zemlji** (ZEM-lyee),

Daj (dye) **nam** (nahm) **danes** (DAH-nes) **naš** (nahsh) **vsakdanji** (FSAHK-dahn-yee) **kruh** (krooh),

in (een) **odpusti** (OHD-poos-tee) **nam** (nahm) **naše** (NAH-sheh) **dolge** (DOHL-geh),

kakor (KAH-kor) **tudi** (TOO-dee) **mi** (mee) **odpuščamo** (OH-dpoosh-CHA-moh) **svojim** (SVOH-yeem) **dolžnikom** (DOHLZH-nee-kom),

In (een) **ne** (neh) **vpelji** (VPEHL-yee) **nas** (nahs) **v** (v) **skušnjavo** (SKOOSH-nah-voh),

temveč (TEHM-vech) **reši** (REH-shee) **nas** (nahs) **hudega** (HOO-deh-gah).

Amen (AH-men).

<u>Understanding the Slovenian Alphabet</u>

Alphabet
- Slovenian uses the **Latin alphabet** with **25 letters**: **A, B, C, Č, D, E, F, G, H, I, J, K, L, M, N, O, P, R, S, Š, T, U, V, Z, Ž**.
- Letters **Q, W, X, Y** appear only in foreign words or names.
- Each letter represents a **distinct sound**, making Slovenian highly phonetic.

Letter Sounds Differ from English
- **A / E / I / O / U** = pure vowels, pronounced as written (dom = dom).
- **Č** = *ch* as in church (čaj = chah-y).
- **Š** = *sh* (šola ≈ shoh-la).
- **Ž** = *zh* as in *measure* (žena ≈ zhe-na).
- **C** = *ts* (cesta = tse-sta).
- **J** = *y* as in yes (jabolko = yah-bol-ko).
- **G** = hard *g* (gora = go-ra).
- **H** = like English *h* (hrana = hra-na).
- **K / L / M / N / P / R / S / T / V / Z** = pronounced roughly as in English, with **R** trilled.
- **D / DZ / DŽ** = D = *d*, Dž = *j* in jump (džem ≈ j-em).
- **Double consonants** = generally pronounced the same as single; no length distinction.

Accent Marks
- Slovenian **does not use accent marks** in standard writing.
- Stress is **dynamic**, usually on the **first syllable of the root**, but can vary.
- Loanwords may retain accents from other languages.

Understanding Slovenian Grammar

Nouns and Gender
- Slovenian has **three genders**: masculine, feminine, neuter.
  - Masculine: *moški* = man.
  - Feminine: *ženska* = woman.
  - Neuter: *otrok* = child.
- Nouns are **declined for six cases**: nominative, genitive, dative, accusative, locative, instrumental.
- Plural endings vary by gender and declension:
  - *moški* → *moški* (man → men).
  - *ženska* → *ženske* (woman→ women).
  - *otrok* → *otroci* (child → children).

Articles
- Slovenian **does not use definite or indefinite articles**; context or demonstratives convey definiteness.

Adjectives
- Agree with nouns in **gender, number, and case**:
  - *nov moški* = new man.
  - *nova ženska* = new woman.
  - *novo otrok* = new child.
- Usually placed **before the noun**.

Pronouns
- Subject: *jaz, ti, on, ona, ono, mi, vi, oni, one, ona.*
- Object: *me, te, ga, jo, nas, vas, jih.*
- Possessive: *moj, tvoj, njegov, njen, naš, vaš, njihov* (declined like adjectives).
- Reflexive: *se.*
- Slovenian is **not pro-drop**, but subject pronouns can often be omitted because verb endings indicate the subject.

Verbs
- Conjugate for **person, number, tense, mood, and aspect**.
- Two aspects: imperfective (ongoing/repeated) and perfective (completed).
- Key tenses:
  - **Present tense:** *jaz govorim* (I speak).

- o **Past tense**: *jaz sem govoril/govorila* (I spoke).
- o **Future tense**: imperfective: *jaz bom govoril/govorila* (I will be speaking), perfective: *jaz bom rekel/rekla* (I will speak).
- Moods: indicative, imperative, conditional.
- Reflexive verbs use *se*: *umivati se* (to wash oneself).

Word Order

- Standard **SVO** (subject-verb-object): *Peter bere knjigo* (Peter reads a book).
- Flexible due to case endings; word order emphasizes focus, contrast, or topic-comment structure.

Questions and Negation

- Yes/No questions use intonation: *Ali govoriš slovensko?* (You speak Slovenian?).
- Question words: *kdo* (who), *kaj* (what), *kje* (where), *kdaj* (when), *zakaj* (why), *kako* (how).
- Negation: *ne* before the verb (*Ne govorim* = I do not speak).

Prepositions

- Govern specific cases (accusative, genitive, dative, locative, instrumental).
- Common: *v* (in), *na* (on), *s/sa* (with), *do* (to), *od* (from), *za* (for).

Special Features

- Slovenian is highly inflected; endings indicate **case, number, and gender**, allowing flexible word order.
- Verb aspect distinguishes completed vs. ongoing actions.
- No articles; definiteness is determined from context or demonstratives.

Chapter XXII

Macedonian

The Lords Prayer in *Македонски* (Macedonian)

Молитва Господова

Наш Оче,
Кој си на небесата,
да се свети Името Твое;
да дојде Царството Твое;
да биде волјата Твоја,
како на небото така и на земјата;
лебот наш насушен дај ни го денес;
и прости ни ги долговите наши,
како што и ние простуваме на нашите
долговници;
и не воведи не во искушение,
туку избави не од злото.
Амин.

Word-to-Word Translation

Молитва Господова (The Our Father)

Наш (Our) **Оче,** (Father,)

Кој (Who) **си** (are) **на** (on) **небесата,** (the heavens,)

да (that/may) **се** (reflexive particle) **свети** (be sanctified) **Името** (the Name) **Твое;** (Your;)

да (that/may) **дојде** (come) **Царството** (the Kingdom) **Твое;** (Your;)

да (that/may) **биде** (be) **волјата** (the Will) **Твоја,** (Your,)

како (as) **на** (on) **небото** (the heaven),

така (so) **и** (also) **на** (on) **земјата;** (the earth;)

лебот (the bread) **наш** (our) **насушен** (daily/necessary) **дај** (give) **ни** (us) **го** (it) **денес;** (today;)

и (and) **прости** (forgive) **ни** (us) **ги** (them) **долговите** (debts) **наши,** (our,)

како (as) **што** (that) **и** (also) **ние** (we) **простуваме** (forgive) **на** (to) **нашите** (our) **долговници;** (debtors;)

и (and) **не** (not) **воведи** (lead) **не** (us) **во** (into) **искушение,** (temptation,)

туку (but) **избави** (deliver/save) **не** (us) **од** (from) **злото.** (evil.)

Амин. (Amen.)

Phonetic Pronunciation

Молитва Господова (MOH-leet-vah GOHS-poh-do-vah)

Наш (nash) Оче (OH-cheh),

Кој (koy) си (see) на (nah) небесата (neh-beh-SAH-tah),

да (dah) се (seh) свети (SVEH-tee) Името (EE-meh-toh) Твое (TVOH-eh);

да (dah) дојде (DOY-deh) Царството (TSAR-stvoh-toh) Твое (TVOH-eh);

да (dah) биде (BEE-deh) волјата (VOH-lyah-tah) Твоја (TVOH-yah),

како (KAH-koh) на (nah) небото (NEH-boh-toh),

така (TAH-kah) и (ee) на (nah) земјата (ZEM-yah-tah);

лебот (LEH-bot) наш (nash) насушен (nah-SOO-shen) дај (dah-ee) ни (nee) го (goh) денес (DEH-nes);

и (ee) прости (PROH-stee) ни (nee) ги (gee) долговите (dol-GOH-vee-teh) наши (NAH-shee),

како (KAH-koh) што (shtoh) и (ee) ние (NEE-eh) простуваме (proh-STOO-vah-meh) на (nah) нашите (NAH-shee-teh) долговници (dol-GOHV-neet-see);

и (ee) не (neh) воведи (VOH-veh-dee) не (neh) во (voh) искушение (ees-koo-SHEH-nyeh),

туку (TOO-koo) избави (eess-BAH-vee) не (neh) од (od) злото (ZLOH-toh).

Амин (AH-meen).

Understanding the Macedonian Alphabet

Alphabet
- Macedonian uses the **Cyrillic alphabet** with **31 letters**:
  А, Б, В, Г, Д, Ѓ, Е, Ж, З, Ѕ, И, Ј, К, Л, Љ, М, Н, Њ, О, П, Р, С, Т, Ќ, У, Ф, Х, Ц, Ч, Џ, Ш.
- Letters **Q, W, X, Y** appear only in foreign words or names.
- Each letter corresponds to a **distinct sound**, making Macedonian highly phonetic.

Letter Sounds Differ from English
- **A / E / I / O / U** = pure vowels, pronounced as written (дом = dom).
- **Ѓ / Ќ** = palatalized *g* and *k* sounds (ѓердан ≈ gjerdan, ќука ≈ kjukja).
- **Ж** = *zh* as in *measure* (жена = zhe-na).
- **Ѕ** = *dz* (ѕвезда ≈ dzv-ehz-da).
- **Ц** = *ts* (цвет = ts-vet).
- **Ч** = *ch* as in church (чаша = cha-sha).
- **Џ** = *j* as in jump (џем = j-em).
- **Ш** = *sh* (школа ≈ sh-ko-la).
- **Ј** = *y* as in yes (јаболко = yah-bol-ko).
- **Г, К, Л, М, Н, П, Р, С, Т, В, Ф, Х** = pronounced roughly as in English; **R** is trilled.
- **Double consonants** = generally pronounced the same as single; lengthening is minor.

Accent Marks
- Macedonian **does not use accent marks** in standard orthography.
- Stress is **dynamic**, usually falling on the antepenultimate or penultimate syllable depending on the word.
- Loanwords may retain accents from other languages.

Understanding Macedonian Grammar

Nouns and Gender
- Macedonian has **three genders**: masculine, feminine, neuter.
  - Masculine: *машки* = man.
  - Feminine: *женски* = woman.
  - Neuter: *неутрален* = child.
- Nouns are **not fully declined for cases** (modern Macedonian uses prepositions more than cases).
- Plural endings vary by gender:
  - *човек* → *луѓе* (man → people).
  - *жена* → *жени* (woman → women).
  - *дете* → *деца* (child → children).

Articles
- Macedonian uses **definite articles as suffixes**:
  - *kniga* = book.
  - *knigata* = the book (definite).
- Indefinite nouns are **bare nouns** (no article).

Adjectives
- Agree with nouns in **gender and number**:
  - *нов човек* = new man.
  - *нова жена* = new woman.
  - *ново дете* = new child.
- Usually placed **before the noun**.

Pronouns
- Subject: *jac, ти, тој, таа, тоа, ние, вие, тие.*
- Object: *ме, те, го, ја, не, ве, ги.*
- Possessive: *мој, твој, негов, нејзин, наш, ваш, нивен* (agree like adjectives).
- Reflexive: *се.*
- Macedonian is **not pro-drop**, but subject pronouns are sometimes omitted.

Verbs
- Conjugate for **person, number, tense, mood, and aspect**.
- Key tenses:
  - Present tense: *jac зборувам* (I speak).

- o **Past (perfect) tense**: *јас зборував* (I spoke / was speaking).
- o **Future tense**: *јас ќе зборувам* (I will speak).
- Moods: indicative, imperative, conditional.
- Aspect (perfective/imperfective) indicates completed vs. ongoing actions.
- Reflexive verbs use *се*: *се мијам* (to wash oneself).

Word Order

- Standard **SVO** (subject-verb-object): *Петар чита книга* (Peter reads a book).
- Flexible due to prepositions and pronouns; emphasis is often indicated by word order.

Questions and Negation

- Yes/No questions use intonation: *Дали зборуваш македонски?* (Do you speak Macedonian?).
- Question words: *Кој* (who), *Што* (what), *Каде* (where), *Кога* (when), *Зошто* (why), *Како* (how).
- Negation: *не* before the verb (*Јас не зборувам* = I do not speak).

Prepositions

- Govern objects, no case endings: *во* (in), *на* (on), *со* (with), *до* (to), *од* (from), *за* (for).

Special Features

- Macedonian is **analytic**, relying on prepositions instead of noun cases.
- Definite articles are **postfixed**.
- Verb aspect and tense are essential to express completed vs. ongoing actions.

Chapter XXIII

Belarusian

The Lords Prayer in *Беларуская* (Belarusian)

Ойча наш

Ойча наш,
які ёсць у нябёсах,
нехай свяціцца імя Тваё;
нехай прыходзіць Валадарства Тваё;
нехай будзе воля Твая,
як на небе, так і на зямлі;
хлеб наш насушны дай нам сёння;
і даруй нам даўгі нашы,
як і мы даруем тым, хто нам даўгі мае;
і не ўводзь нас у спакусу,
але выратоўвай нас ад злога.
Амін.

Word-to-Word Translation

Ойча наш (The Our Father)

Ойча (Father) **наш,** (our,)

якí (who) **ёсць** (is) **у** (in) **нябёсах,** (heavens,)

нехай (let/may) **ся** (reflexive particle) **свяціцца** (be sanctified) **імя** (name) **Тваё;** (your;)

нехай (let/may) **прыходзіць** (come) **Валадарства** (kingdom) **Тваё;** (your;)

нехай (let/may) **будзе** (be) **воля** (will) **Твая,** (your,)

як (as) **на** (on) **небе,** (heaven,)

так (so) **і** (also) **на** (on) **зямлі;** (earth;)

хлеб (bread) **наш** (our) **насушны** (daily) **дай** (give) **нам** (us) **сёння;** (today;)

і (and) **даруй** (forgive) **нам** (us) **даўгі** (debts) **нашы,** (our,)

як (as) **і** (also) **мы** (we) **даруем** (forgive) **тым,** (those,)

хто (who) **нам** (to us) **даўгі** (debts) **мае;** (have;)

і (and) **не** (not) **ўводзь** (lead) **нас** (us) **у** (into) **спакусу,** (temptation,)

але (but) **выратоўвай** (deliver) **нас** (us) **ад** (from) **злога.** (evil.)

Амін. (Amen.)

Phonetic Pronunciation

Ойча наш (OY-chah nash)

Ойча (OY-chah) наш (nash),

які (YAH-kee) ёсць (yosts') у (oo) нябёсах (nya-BYOH-sahkh),

нехай (NEH-khay) ся (sya) свяціцца (SVYA-tsee-tsah) імя (EE-mya) Тваё (TVAH-yo);

нехай (NEH-khay) прыходзіць (pri-KHO-dzeet) Валадарства (vah-lah-DAR-stvah) Тваё (TVAH-yo);

нехай (NEH-khay) будзе (BOO-dzeh) воля (VOH-lya) Твая (TVAH-ya),

як (yahk) на (nah) небе (NEH-beh),

так (tahk) і (ee) на (nah) зямлі (ZYAM-lee);

хлеб (khleb) наш (nash) насушны (nah-SOOSH-ny) дай (dah-ee) нам (nahm) сёння (SNYOH-nyah);

і (ee) даруй (DAR-oo-ee) нам (nahm) даўгі (DAU-ghee) нашы (NAH-shee),

як (yahk) і (ee) мы (mih) даруем (DAR-oo-yehm) тым (tym), хто (khto) нам (nahm) даўгі (DAU-ghee) мае (MAH-yeh);

і (ee) не (nyeh) ўводзь (OO-vodz') нас (nahs) у (oo) спакусу (spah-KOO-soo),

але (AH-leh) выратоўвай (vy-rah-TOHV-vay) нас (nahs) ад (ahd) злога (ZLOH-gah).

Амін (AH-meen).

Understanding the Belarusian Alphabet

Alphabet

- Belarusian uses the **Cyrillic alphabet** with **32 letters**: А, Б, В, Г, Д, Е, Ё, Ж, З, І, Й, К, Л, М, Н, О, П, Р, С, Т, У, Ў, Ф, Х, Ц, Ч, Ш, Ы, Ь, Э, Ю, Я, Ґ.
- Letters **Q, W, X, Y** appear only in foreign words or names.
- Each letter corresponds to a **distinct sound**, making Belarusian highly phonetic.

Letter Sounds Differ from English

- **A / E / I / O / U** = pure vowels, pronounced as written (дом = dom).
- **Ё** = *yo* (сёстры = syostry).
- **І** = *ee* as in machine (місто = meesto).
- **Ў** = semi-vowel like English *w* (ўвесь ≈ w-ves).
- **Ж** = *zh* as in *measure* (жыццё = zhi-tsyo).
- **Ц** = *ts* (царква ≈ tsark-va).
- **Ч** = *ch* as in church (час = chas).
- **Ш** = *sh* (школа ≈ shko-la).
- **Г / Ґ** = G = hard *g* (горад = go-rad); Ґ = slightly stronger *g* in loanwords.
- **Й** = *y* as in yes (йогурт = yo-gurt).
- **Л / М / Н / П / Р / С / Т / Ф / Х / В / Д / З** = pronounced roughly as in English; **R** is trilled.
- **Double consonants** = generally pronounced the same as single; lengthening is minor.

Accent Marks

- Belarusian **does not use accent marks** in standard writing.
- Stress is **dynamic**, usually not indicated, and can fall on different syllables depending on the word.
- Loanwords may retain accents from other languages.

Understanding Belarusian Grammar

Nouns and Gender
- Belarusian has **three genders**: masculine, feminine, neuter.
    - Masculine: *чалавек* = man.
    - Feminine: *жанчына* = woman.
    - Neuter: *дзіця* = child.
- Nouns are **declined for seven cases**: nominative, genitive, dative, accusative, instrumental, locative, vocative.
- Plural endings vary by gender and declension:
    - *чалавек* → *людзі* (man → people).
    - *жанчына* → *жанчыны* (woman → women).
    - *дзіця* → *дзеці* (child → children).

Articles
- Belarusian **does not use definite or indefinite articles**; context conveys definiteness.

Adjectives
- Agree with nouns in **gender, number, and case**:
    - *новы чалавек* = new man.
    - *новая жанчына* = new woman.
    - *новае дзіця* = new child.
- Usually placed **before the noun**.

Pronouns
- Subject: *я, ты, ён, яна, яно, мы, вы, яны*.
- Object: *мяне, цябе, яго, яе, нас, вас, іх*.
- Possessive: *мой, твая, яго, яе, наш, ваш, іх* (declined like adjectives).
- Reflexive: *сябе*.
- Belarusian is **not pro-drop**, but subject pronouns can sometimes be omitted due to verb endings.

Verbs
- Conjugate for **person, number, tense, mood, and aspect**.
- Two aspects: imperfective (ongoing/repeated) and perfective (completed).
- Key tenses:
    - **Present tense**: *я кажу* (I speak).
    - **Past tense**: *я сказаў/сказала* (I spoke).

- ○ **Future tense**: imperfective: *я буду казаць* (I will be speaking), perfective: *я скажу* (I will speak).
- Moods: indicative, imperative, conditional.
- Reflexive verbs use *сябе*: *мыць сябе* (to wash oneself).

Word Order
- Standard **SVO** (subject-verb-object): *Пётр чытае кнігу* (Peter reads a book).
- Flexible due to case endings; emphasis or contrast is often shown by word order.

Questions and Negation
- Yes/No questions use intonation: *Ці ты гаворыш па-беларуску?* (Do you speak Belarusian?).
- Question words: *Хто* (who), *Што* (what), *Дзе* (where), *Калі* (when), *Чаму* (why), *Як* (how).
- Negation: *не* before the verb (*Я не кажу* = I do not speak).

Prepositions
- Govern specific cases (accusative, genitive, dative, instrumental, locative).
- Common: *у* (in), *на* (on), *з* (with), *да* (to), *ад* (from), *для* (for).

Special Features
- Belarusian is highly inflected; endings indicate **case, number, and gender**, allowing flexible word order.
- Verb aspect is essential to distinguish completed vs. ongoing actions.
- No articles; definiteness is determined from context or demonstratives.

Chapter XXIV

Ukrainian

The Lords Prayer in *Українська* (Ukrainian)

Отче наш

Отче наш,
що є на небесах,
нехай святиться ім'я Твоє;
нехай прийде Царство Твоє;
нехай буде воля Твоя,
як на небі, так і на землі;
хліб наш насущний дай нам сьогодні;
і прости нам провини наші,
як і ми прощаємо винуватцям нашим;
і не введи нас у спокусу,
але визволи нас від лукавого.
Амінь.

Word-to-Word Translation

Отче наш (The Our Father)

Отче (Father) **наш,** (our,)

що (who/that) є (is) на (on) небесах, (heavens,)

нехай (let/may) святиться (be sanctified) ім'я (name) Твоє;
(Your;)

нехай (let/may) прийде (come) Царство (kingdom) Твоє;
(Your;)

нехай (let/may) буде (be) воля (will) Твоя, (Your,)

як (as) на (on) небі, (heaven,)

так (so) і (also) на (on) землі; (earth;)

хліб (bread) наш (our) насущний (daily) дай (give) нам (us)
сьогодні; (today;)

і (and) прости (forgive) нам (us) провини (sins/faults) наші,
(our,)

як (as) і (also) ми (we) прощаємо (forgive) винуватцям (guilty
ones) нашим; (our;)

і (and) не (not) введи (lead) нас (us) у (into) спокусу,
(temptation,)

але (but) визволи (deliver) нас (us) від (from) лукавого. (evil
one.)

Амінь. (Amen.)

Phonetic Pronunciation

Отче наш (OT-cheh nash)

Отче (OT-cheh) **наш** (nash),

що (shcho) **є** (ye) **на** (nah) **небесах** (neh-beh-SAHkh),

нехай (NEH-khay) **святиться** (SVYA-tee-tsya) **ім'я** (IM-ya) **Твоє** (TVOH-yeh);

нехай (NEH-khay) **прийде** (pri-YDEH) **Царство** (TSAR-stvo) **Твоє** (TVOH-yeh);

нехай (NEH-khay) **буде** (BOO-deh) **воля** (VOH-lya) **Твоя** (TVOH-ya),

як (yahk) **на** (nah) **небі** (NEH-bee)

так (tahk) **і** (ee) **на** (nah) **землі** (zem-LEE);

хліб (khleeb) **наш** (nash) **насущний** (nah-SOOSH-ny) **дай** (dah-ee) **нам** (nahm) **сьогодні** (s'OH-ho-dnee);

і (ee) **прости** (PROH-stee) **нам** (nahm) **провини** (proh-VEE-ny) **наші** (NAH-shee),

як (yahk) **і** (ee) **ми** (my) **прощаємо** (proh-shchah-YEH-mo) **винуватцям** (vee-noo-VAHT-syam) **нашім** (NAH-sheem);

і (ee) **не** (nyeh) **веди** (VEH-dee) **нас** (nahs) **у** (oo) **спокусу** (spoh-KOO-soo),

але (AH-leh) **визволи** (veez-VOH-lee) **нас** (nahs) **від** (veed) **лукавого** (loo-KAH-voh-ho).

Амінь (AH-meen).

Understanding the Ukrainian Alphabet

Alphabet

- Ukrainian uses the **Cyrillic alphabet** with **33 letters**:
  А, Б, В, Г, Ґ, Д, Е, Є, Ж, З, И, І, Ї, Й, К, Л, М, Н, О, П, Р, С, Т, У, Ф, Х, Ц, Ч, Ш, Щ, Ь, Ю, Я.
- Letters **Q, W, X, Y** appear only in foreign words or names.
- Each letter corresponds to a **distinct sound**, making Ukrainian highly phonetic.

Letter Sounds Differ from English

- **A / E / I / O / U** = pure vowels, pronounced as written (дім = dim).
- **Є** = *ye* (енот ≈ ye-not).
- **Ї** = *yi* (їжак ≈ yi-zhak).
- **Ґ** = hard *g* (ранок ≈ ganok); **Г** = softer *h* sound (гора ≈ hora).
- **И** = like Russian *i* but more central (син = sin).
- **Й** = *y* as in yes (йога ≈ yo-ga).
- **Ж** = *zh* as in *measure* (жінка ≈ zhi-nka).
- **Ц** = *ts* (цукор ≈ tsu-kor).
- **Ч** = *ch* as in church (чай ≈ chay).
- **Ш** = *sh* (школа ≈ sh-ko-la).
- **Щ** = *shch* (щастя ≈ shchast-ya).
- **Ю** = *yu* (юнак ≈ yu-nak).
- **Я** = *ya* (яблуко ≈ ya-blu-ko).
- **Л / М / Н / П / Р / С / Т / Ф / Х / В / Д / З** = pronounced roughly as in English; **R** is trilled.
- **Double consonants** = generally pronounced the same as single; lengthening is minor.

Accent Marks

- Ukrainian **does not use accent marks** in standard writing.
- Stress is **dynamic** and can fall on different syllables depending on the word.
- Loanwords may retain accents from other languages.

Understanding Ukrainian Grammar

Nouns and Gender
- Ukrainian has **three genders**: masculine, feminine, neuter.
  - Masculine: *чоловік* = man.
  - Feminine: *жінка* = woman.
  - Neuter: *дитя* = child.
- Nouns decline for **seven cases**: nominative, genitive, dative, accusative, instrumental, locative, vocative.
- Plural formation depends on noun class:
  - *чоловік* → *чоловіки* (man → men).
  - *жінка* → *жінки* (woman → women).
  - *дитя* → *діти* (child → children).

Articles
- Ukrainian **does not use definite or indefinite articles**; context or demonstratives (*цей, та, ті*) conveys definiteness.

Adjectives
- Agree with nouns in **gender, number, and case**.
  - *новий чоловік* = new man.
  - *нова жінка* = new woman.
  - *нове дитя* = new child.
- Normally placed **before the noun**.

Pronouns
- Subject: *я, ти, він, вона, воно, ми, ви, вони.*
- Object: *мене, тебе, його, її, нас, вас, їх.*
- Possessive: *мій, твій, його, її, наш, ваш, їх* (decline like adjectives).
- Reflexive: *себе.*
- Ukrainian is **not strictly pro-drop**, but subject pronouns may be omitted because verb endings mark person.

Verbs
- Conjugated for **person, number, tense, mood, and aspect**.
- Aspects: **imperfective** (ongoing/repeated) vs. **perfective** (completed).
- Key tenses:
  - **Present tense**: *я говорю* (I speak).
  - **Past tense**: *я говорив/говорила* (I spoke).

- o **Future tense**: imperfective: *я буду говорити* (I will be speaking); perfective: *я скажу* (I will say).
- Moods: indicative, imperative, conditional (*я сказав би* = I would say).
- Reflexive verbs: *-ся/-сь*: *вчитися* = to study (oneself).

Word Order

- Default **SVO** (subject-verb-object): *Олег читає книжку* (Oleg reads a book).
- Word order is flexible due to rich case system, often used for emphasis or style.

Questions and Negation

- Yes/No questions use intonation: *Ти говориш українською?* (You speak Ukrainian?).
- Question words: *Хто* (who), *Що* (what), *Де* (where), *Коли* (when), *Чому* (why), *Як* (how).
- Negation: *не* before the verb (*Я не говорю* = I do not speak).

Prepositions

- Govern specific cases (genitive, accusative, dative, instrumental, locative).
- Common: *в/у* (in), *на* (on), *з* (with/from), *до* (to), *від* (from), *для* (for).

Special Features

- Highly inflected: endings show **case, number, gender**.
- Verb aspect is key to expressing action meaning.
- Distinctive **vocative case** used in direct address (*друже!* = friend!).
- Stress shifts can change meaning or form.

Chapter XXV

Russian

The Lords Prayer in *Русский* (Russian)

Отче наш

Отче наш,
Иже еси на небесех,
да святится имя Твое;
да приидет Царствие Твое;
да будет воля Твоя,
яко на небеси и на земли;
хлеб наш насущный дай нам днесь;
и остави нам долги наша,
якоже и мы оставляем должником нашим;
и не введи нас во искушение,
но избави нас от лукаваго.
Аминь.

Word-to-Word Translation

Отче наш (The Our Father)

Отче (Father) наш, (our,)

Иже (who) еси (are) на (on) небесех, (heavens,)

да (let/may) святится (be sanctified) имя (name) Твое; (Your;)

да (let/may) приидет (come) Царствие (kingdom) Твое; (Your;)

да (let/may) будет (be) воля (will) Твоя, (Your,)

яко (as) на (on) небеси (heaven) и (and) на (on) земли; (earth;)

хлеб (bread) наш (our) насущный (daily) дай (give) нам (us) днесь; (today;)

и (and) остави (forgive/leave) нам (us) долги (debts) наша, (our,)

якоже (as) и (also) мы (we) оставляем (forgive/leave) должником (debtors) нашим; (our;)

и (and) не (not) введи (lead) нас (us) во (into) искушение, (temptation,)

но (but) избави (deliver) нас (us) от (from) лукавого. (evil one.)

Аминь. (Amen.)

Phonetic Pronunciation

Отче наш (OT-cheh nash)

Отче (OT-cheh) наш (nash),

Иже (EE-zheh) еси (ye-SEE) на (nah) небесех (nyeh-beh-SEHkh),

да (dah) святится (svya-TEE-tsa) имя (EE-mya) Твое (tvo-YEH);

да (dah) приидет (pree-EE-det) Царствие (TSAR-stvee-yeh) Твое (tvo-YEH);

да (dah) будет (BOO-det) воля (VOH-lya) Твоя (tvo-YAH),

яко (YA-ko) на (nah) небеси (nyeh-be-SEE) и (ee) на (nah) земли (zyehm-LEE);

хлеб (khlyeb) наш (nash) насущный (nah-SOOSH-ny) дай (day) нам (nahm) днесь (dnyes');

и (ee) остави (ah-STAH-vee) нам (nahm) долги (dahl-GHEE) наша (NAH-sha),

якоже (YA-ko-zheh) и (ee) мы (my) оставляем (ah-stahv-LYAH-yem) должником (dahl-zhnee-KOHM) нашим (NAH-sheem);

и (ee) не (nyeh) введи (vve-DEE) нас (nahs) во (vo) искушение (ees-koo-SHEH-nee-yeh),

но (noh) избави (eez-BAH-vee) нас (nahs) от (oht) лукавого (loo-KAH-vah-voh).

Аминь (ah-MEEN).

147

Understanding the Russian Alphabet

Alphabet
- Russian uses the **Cyrillic alphabet** with **33 letters**:
  А, Б, В, Г, Д, Е, Ё, Ж, З, И, Й, К, Л, М, Н, О, П, Р, С, Т, У, Ф, Х, Ц, Ч, Ш, Щ, Ъ, Ы, Ь, Э, Ю, Я.
- Letters **Q, W, X, Y** appear only in foreign words or names.
- Each letter corresponds to a **distinct sound**, making Russian highly phonetic.

Letter Sounds Differ from English
- **А / Е / И / О / У / Ы / Э** = pure vowels, pronounced as written (дом = dom).
- **Ё** = *yo* (ёлка ≈ yo-lka).
- **Ю** = *yu* (юг ≈ yug).
- **Я** = *ya* (яблоко ≈ ya-blo-ko).
- **Й** = *y* as in yes (йогурт ≈ yo-gurt).
- **Ж** = *zh* as in *measure* (жена ≈ zhe-na).
- **Ц** = *ts* (царь ≈ tsar).
- **Ч** = *ch* as in church (чай ≈ chay).
- **Ш** = *sh* (школа ≈ sh-ko-la).
- **Щ** = *shch* (щука ≈ shchu-ka).
- **Г** = hard *g* (город = go-rod).
- **Х** = like German *ch* or Scottish *loch* (хлеб ≈ khleb).
- **Л / М / Н / П / Р / С / Т / Ф / В / Д / З** = pronounced roughly as in English; **R** is trilled.
- **Ъ (hard sign)** = no sound; separates consonants from following soft vowels.
- **Ь (soft sign)** = softens preceding consonant.
- **Double consonants** = generally pronounced the same as single; lengthening is minor.

Accent Marks
- Russian **does not usually write accents**.
- Stress is **dynamic**, often falling on different syllables depending on the word, and must be learned.
- Loanwords may retain accents from other languages.

Understanding Russian Grammar

Nouns and Gender
- Russian has **three genders**: masculine, feminine, neuter.
  - o   Masculine: *мужчина* = man.
  - o   Feminine: *женщина* = woman.
  - o   Neuter: *ребёнок* = child.
- Nouns are **declined for six cases**: nominative, genitive, dative, accusative, instrumental, prepositional.
- Plural formation varies by gender and noun type:
  - o   *мужчина → мужчины* (man → men).
  - o   *женщина → женщины* (woman → women).
  - o   *ребёнок → дети* (child → children).

Articles
- Russian **does not use definite or indefinite articles**; definiteness is inferred from context or demonstratives (*этот, та, те*).

Adjectives
- Agree with nouns in **gender, number, and case**:
  - o   *новый мужчина* = new man.
  - o   *новая женщина* = new woman.
  - o   *новое ребёнок* = new child.
- Usually placed **before the noun**.

Pronouns
- Subject: *я, ты, он, она, оно, мы, вы, они.*
- Object: *меня, тебя, его, её, нас, вас, их.*
- Possessive: *мой, твой, его, её, наш, ваш, их* (declined like adjectives).
- Reflexive: *себя.*
- Russian is **not pro-drop**, though subject pronouns can be omitted because verb endings indicate person.

Verbs
- Conjugate for **person, number, tense, mood, and aspect**.
- Aspects: **imperfective** (ongoing/repeated) vs. **perfective** (completed).
- Key tenses:
  - o   **Present tense(imperfective only):** *я говорю* (I speak).
  - o   **Past tense:** *я говорил/говорила* (I spoke).

- o **Future tense**: imperfective: *я буду говорить* (I will be speaking); perfective: *я скажу* (I will say).
- Moods: indicative, imperative, conditional (*я бы сказал* = I would say).
- Reflexive verbs use *-ся*: *учиться* = to study (oneself).

Word Order
- Standard **SVO** (subject-verb-object): *Пётр читает книгу* (Peter reads a book).
- Flexible due to case system; word order often conveys emphasis or contrast.

Questions and Negation
- Yes/No questions use intonation: *Ты говоришь по-русски?* (You speak in Russian?).
- Question words: *Кто* (who), *Что* (what), *Где* (where), *Когда* (when), *Почему* (why), *Как* (how).
- Negation: *не* before the verb (*Я не говорю* = I do not speak).
- Double negation is standard: *Я ничего не знаю* (I know nothing).

Prepositions
- Govern specific cases: *в/во* (in), *на* (on), *с* (with/from), *к* (to), *от* (from), *для* (for).

Special Features
- Highly inflected: endings indicate **case, number, and gender**.
- Verb aspect is crucial for distinguishing completed vs. ongoing actions.
- Stress placement can shift meaning or conjugation form.
- Russian has **no articles**, unlike many Western European languages.

Chapter XXVI

Latvian

The Lords Prayer in *Latviešu* (Latvian)

Mūsu Tēvs

Mūsu Tēvs,
kas esi debesīs,
svētīts lai top Tavs vārds;
lai nāk Tavs valstība;
lai top Tavs prāts,
kā debesīs, tā uz zemes;
dod mums šodien mūsu ikdienas maizi;
piedod mums mūsu parādus,
kā arī mēs piedodam saviem parādniekiem;
un nepārnes mūs kārdināšanā,
bet atpestī mūs no ļaunā.
Āmen.

Word-to-Word Translation

Mūsu Tēvs (The Our Father)

Mūsu (Our) Tēvs, (Father,)

kas (who) esi (are) debesīs, (in heavens,)

svētīts (blessed) lai (let) top (become) Tavs (Your) vārds; (name;)

lai (let) nāk (come) Tavs (Your) valstība; (kingdom;)

lai (let) top (become) Tavs (Your) prāts, (will,)

kā (as) debesīs, (in heavens,)

tā (so) uz (on) zemes; (earth;)

dod (give) mums (us) šodien (today) mūsu (our) ikdienas (daily) maizi; (bread;)

piedod (forgive) mums (us) mūsu (our) parādus, (debts,)

kā (as) arī (also) mēs (we) piedodam (forgive) saviem (our) parādniekiem; (debtors;)

un (and) nepārnes (do not lead) mūs (us) kārdināšanā, (into temptation,)

bet (but) atpestī (deliver) mūs (us) no (from) ļaunā. (evil.)

Āmen. (Amen.)

Phonetic Pronunciation

Mūsu Tēvs (MOO-soo TEH-vs)

Mūsu (MOO-soo) Tēvs (TEH-vs),

kas (kahs) esi (EH-see) debesīs (DEH-beh-sees),

svētīts (SVEH-teets) lai (lai) top (tohp) Tavs (tahvs) vārds (vahrds);

lai (lai) nāk (nahhk) Tava (TAH-vah) valstība (VAHL-stee-bah);

lai (lai) top (tohp) Tavs (tahvs) prāts (prahts),

kā (kah) debesīs (DEH-beh-sees),

tā (tah) uz (oos) zemes (ZEH-mess);

dod (dohd) mums (mooms) šodien (SHOH-dyen) mūsu (MOO-soo) ikdienas (EEK-dyeh-nahs) maizi (MAI-zee);

piedod (PYEH-dohd) mums (mooms) mūsu (MOO-soo) parādus (PAH-rah-doos),

kā (kah) arī (AH-ree) mēs (mehhs) piedodam (PYEH-doh-dahm) saviem (SAH-vyehm) parādniekiem (PAH-rahd-nyeh-kyehm);

un (oon) nepārnes (NEH-pahr-ness) mūs (moos) kārdināšanā (KAHR-dee-nah-shah-nah),

bet (beht) atpestī (AHT-peh-stee) mūs (moos) no (noh) ļaunā (L'YAU-nah).

Āmen. (AH-men).

Understanding the Latvian Alphabet

Alphabet
- Latvian uses the **Latin alphabet** with **33 letters**, including diacritics: **A, Ā, B, C, Č, D, E, Ē, F, G, Ģ, H, I, Ī, J, K, Ķ, L, Ļ, M, N, Ņ, O, P, R, S, Š, T, U, Ū, V, Z, Ž**.
- Letters **Q, W, X, Y** appear only in foreign words or names.
- Each letter represents a **distinct sound**, making Latvian highly phonetic.

Letter Sounds Differ from English
- **A / Ā** = short and long *ah* (sāls ≈ saahls).
- **E / Ē** = short and long *eh* (elektrība ≈ eh-lek-tree-bah).
- **I / Ī** = short and long *ee* (sīks ≈ see-ks).
- **O / U / Ū** = *o, oo* (ūdens ≈ oo-dens).
- **C** = *ts* (cits ≈ tsits).
- **Č** = *ch* as in church (četras ≈ cheh-tras).
- **Š** = *sh* (šaha ≈ shaha).
- **Ž** = *zh* as in *measure* (žurnāls ≈ zhur-nahls).
- **G / Ģ** = G = hard *g* (gars ≈ gars); Ģ = soft *g* (ģimene ≈ gyim-eh-neh).
- **K / Ķ** = K = hard *k* (katrs ≈ katrs); Ķ = palatalized *k* (ķēķis ≈ kyehk-is).
- **L / Ļ** = L = as in English; Ļ = palatalized *l* (ļoti ≈ l-yoti).
- **N / Ņ** = N = as in English; Ņ = palatalized *n* (ņem ≈ nyehm).
- **J** = *y* as in yes (jauns ≈ yah-uns).
- **R** = trilled.
- **Double consonants** = pronounced slightly longer: kanna (kah-nnah) vs. kana (kah-nah).

Accent Marks
- Latvian uses **macrons (ā, ē, ī, ū)** to indicate vowel length.
- Stress is **usually on the first syllable** of a word.
- Loanwords may retain accents from other languages.

Understanding Latvian Grammar

Nouns and Gender
- Latvian has **two genders**: masculine and feminine.
  - Masculine: *vīrietis* = man.
  - Feminine: *sieviete* = woman.
- Nouns are **declined for seven cases**: nominative, genitive, dative, accusative, instrumental, locative, vocative.
- Plural forms vary by gender and declension:
  - *vīrietis* → *vīrieši* (man → men).
  - *sieviete* → *sievietes* (woman → women).

Articles
- Latvian **does not use definite or indefinite articles**; definiteness is inferred from context or demonstratives (*šis, tā, tie*).

Adjectives
- Agree with nouns in **gender, number, and case**:
  - *jauns vīrietis* = young man.
  - *jauna sieviete* = young woman.
- Usually placed **before the noun**.

Pronouns
- Subject: *es, tu, viņš, viņa, mēs, jūs, viņi/viņas*.
- Object: *mani, tevi, viņu, mūs, jūs, viņus/viņas*.
- Possessive: *mans, tava, viņa, mūsu, jūsu, viņu* (declined like adjectives).
- Reflexive: *sevi*.
- Latvian is **not pro-drop**, though subject pronouns can be omitted when verb endings are clear.

Verbs
- Conjugated for **person, number, tense, mood, and aspect**.
- Tenses:
  - **Present tense**: *es runāju* (I speak).
  - **Past tense**: *es runāju* (I spoke).
  - **Future tense**: *es runāšu* (I will speak).
- Moods: indicative, imperative, conditional (*es runātu* = I would speak).
- Verbs do not have a strong grammatical aspect distinction like Slavic languages.

Latvian ~ The Lords Prayer

Word Order
- Standard **SVO** (subject-verb-object): *Jānis lasa grāmatu* (Janis reads a book).
- Flexible due to case endings; word order emphasizes focus or contrast.

Questions and Negation
- Yes/No questions use intonation: *Tu runā latviski?* (You speak in Latvian?).
- Question words: *Kas* (who/what), *Kur* (where), *Kad* (when), *Kāpēc* (why), *Kā* (how).
- Negation: *ne* before the verb (*Es nerunāju* = I do not speak).

Prepositions
- Govern specific cases (usually genitive, dative, accusative).
- Common: *uz* (on), *ar* (with), *pie* (at), *no* (from), *priekš* (for).

Special Features
- Rich inflection system: endings indicate **case, number, gender**.
- Vocative case is used in direct address (*draugs!* = friend!).
- Stress is usually predictable but can vary by word.
- No articles; definiteness is expressed with context or demonstratives.

Chapter XXVII

Lithuanian

The Lords Prayer in *Lietuvių* (Lithuanian)

Tėve mūsų

Tėve mūsų,
Kuris esi danguje,
Tebūna šventas Tavo vardas;
Tebūna Tavo karalystė;
Tebūna Tavo valia,
Kaip danguje, taip ir žemėje.
Duok mums šiandien mūsų kasdienį duoną;
Atleisk mums mūsų kaltes,
Kaip ir mes atleidžiame savo kaltininkams;
Ir nevesk mūsų į pagundą,
Bet gelbėk mus nuo pikto.
Amen.

Word-to-Word Translation

Tėve mūsų (The Our Father)

Tėve (Father) mūsų (our),

Kuris (who) esi (are) danguje (in heaven),

Tebūna (let be) šventas (holy) Tavo (Your) vardas (name);

Tebūna (let be) Tavo (Your) karalystė (kingdom);

Tebūna (let be) Tavo (Your) valia (will),

Kaip (as) danguje (in heaven),

taip (so) ir (also) žemėje (on earth).

Duok (Give) mums (us) šiandien (today) mūsų (our) kasdienį
(daily) duoną (bread);

Atleisk (forgive) mums (us) mūsų (our) kaltes (debts/sins),

Kaip (as) ir (also) mes (we) atleidžiame (forgive) savo (our)
kaltininkams (debtors);

Ir (and) nevesk (do not lead) mūsų (us) į (into) pagundą
(temptation),

Bet (but) gelbėk (deliver/save) mus (us) nuo (from) pikto (evil).

Amen (Amen).

Phonetic Pronunciation

Tėve mūsų (TEH-veh MOO-soo)

Tėve (TEH-veh) mūsų (MOO-soo),

Kuris (KOO-rees) esi (EH-see) danguje (DAHN-goo-yeh),

Tebūna (teh-BOO-nah) šventas (SHVEHN-tahs) Tavo (TAH-voh)
vardas (VAR-dahs);

Tebūna (teh-BOO-nah) Tavo (TAH-voh) karalystė (kah-rah-
LEES-teh);

Tebūna (teh-BOO-nah) Tavo (TAH-voh) valia (VAH-lyah),

Kaip (kaipe) danguje (DAHN-goo-yeh),

taip (taipe) ir (eer) žemėje (ZHEH-meh-yeh).

Duok (dwok) mums (mooms) šiandien (SHEE-ahn-dyen) mūsų
(MOO-soo) kasdienį (kahs-DYEH-nee) duoną (DWOO-nah);

Atleisk (aht-LAYSK) mums (mooms) mūsų (MOO-soo) kaltes
(kahl-TEHS),

Kaip (kaipe) ir (eer) mes (mehs) atleidžiame (aht-LAY-dzhah-meh)
savo (SAH-voh) kaltininkams (kahl-tee-NEEN-kahms);

Ir (eer) nevesk (neh-VESK) mūsų (MOO-soo) į (ee) pagundą (pah-
GOON-dah),

Bet (beht) gelbėk (GEL-bek) mus (moos) nuo (NOO-oh) pikto
(PEEK-toh).

Amen (AH-mehn).

Understanding the Lithuanian Alphabet

Alphabet

- Lithuanian uses the **Latin alphabet** with **32 letters**, including diacritics: A, Ą, B, C, Č, D, E, Ę, Ė, F, G, H, I, Į, Y, J, K, L, M, N, O, P, R, S, Š, T, U, Ų, Ū, V, Z, Ž.
- Letters **Q, W, X** appear only in foreign words or names.
- Each letter corresponds to a **distinct sound**, making Lithuanian highly phonetic.

Letter Sounds Differ from English

- **A / Ą** = short and long *ah* (sąsiuvinis ≈ saah-syu-vi-nis).
- **E / Ę / Ė** = short, nasal, and long *eh* (ėsti ≈ eh-sti).
- **I / Į / Y** = short and long *ee* (įdomu ≈ ee-doh-moo, ypač ≈ ee-pahch).
- **O / U / Ų / Ū** = short, nasal, and long vowels (ūdra ≈ oo-drah).
- **C** = *ts* (citrina ≈ tsit-ree-na).
- **Č** = *ch* as in church (čia ≈ chya).
- **Š** = *sh* (šuo ≈ shoo-oh).
- **Ž** = *zh* as in *measure* (žmogus ≈ zhmoh-gus).
- **G** = hard *g* (geras ≈ geh-ras).
- **J** = *y* as in yes (jaunas ≈ yah-oo-nas).
- **R** = trilled.
- **L / M / N / P / S / T / V / D / H / K / Z** = pronounced roughly as in English.
- **Double consonants** = generally pronounced the same as single; lengthening is minor.

Accent Marks

- Lithuanian uses **diacritics** (macrons, ogoneks, dots) primarily to indicate vowel length and quality.
- Stress is **dynamic**, usually falling on the first, second, or penultimate syllable, depending on the word.
- Loanwords may retain accents from other languages.

Understanding Lithuanian Grammar

Nouns and Gender
- Lithuanian has **two genders**: masculine and feminine.
  - Masculine: *vyras* = man.
  - Feminine: *moteris* = woman.
- Nouns are **declined for seven cases**: nominative, genitive, dative, accusative, instrumental, locative, vocative.
- Plural formation depends on noun endings:
  - *vyras* → *vyrai* (man → men).
  - *moteris* → *moterys* (woman → women).

Articles
- Lithuanian **does not use definite or indefinite articles**; definiteness is inferred from context or demonstratives (*tas, ši, tie*).

Adjectives
- Agree with nouns in **gender, number, and case**:
  - *jaunas vyras* = young man.
  - *jauna moteris* = young woman.
- Usually placed **before the noun**.

Pronouns
- Subject: *aš, tu, jis, ji, mes, jūs, jie/jos*.
- Object: *mane, tave, jį, ją, mus, jus, juos/jas*.
- Possessive: *mano, tavo, jo, jos, mūsų, jūsų, jų*.
- Reflexive: *save*.
- Lithuanian is **not pro-drop**, but subject pronouns can be omitted when verb endings clearly indicate person.

Verbs
- Conjugated for **person, number, tense, mood, and aspect**.
- Key tenses:
  - **Present tense**: *aš kalbu* (I speak).
  - **Past tense**: *aš kalbėjau* (I spoke).
  - **Future tense**: *aš kalbėsiu* (I will speak).
- Moods: indicative, imperative, conditional (*aš kalbėčiau* = I would speak).
- Verbs do not have strict perfective/imperfective distinction like Slavic languages.

Lithuanian ~ The Lords Prayer

Word Order
- Standard **SVO** (subject-verb-object): *Jonas skaito knygą* (Jonas reads a book).
- Flexible due to case endings; word order often marks emphasis or contrast.

Questions and Negation
- Yes/No questions use intonation: *Ar tu kalbi lietuviškai?* (Do you speak Lithuanian?).
- Question words: *Kas* (who/what), *Kur* (where), *Kada* (when), *Kodėl* (why), *Kaip* (how).
- Negation: *ne* before the verb (*Aš nekalbu* = I do not speak).

Prepositions
- Govern specific cases (genitive, accusative, dative, instrumental, locative).
- Common: *ant* (on), *su* (with), *prie* (at), *iš* (from), *dėl* (because of/for).

Special Features
- Highly inflected: endings show **case, number, and gender**.
- Vocative case used in direct address (*drauge!* = friend!).
- Stress is generally predictable but can vary for emphasis.
- No articles; definiteness expressed via context or demonstratives.

Chapter XXVIII

Finnish

The Lords Prayer in *Suomi* (Finnish)

Isä meidän

Isä meidän,
joka olet taivaissa,
pyhitetty olkoon sinun nimesi;
tulkoon sinun valtakuntasi;
tapahtukoon sinun tahtosi,
niin kuin taivaassa, niin myös maan päällä.
Anna meille tänä päivänä meidän jokapäiväinen
leipämme;
ja anna meille meidän velkamme anteeksi,
niin kuin mekin annamme anteeksi velallisillemme;
äläkä saata meitä kiusaukseen,
vaan päästä meidät pahasta.
Aamen.

Word-to-Word Translation

Isä meidän (The Our Father)

Isä (Father) meidän (our),

joka (who) olet (are) taivaissa (in heavens),

pyhitetty (sanctified) olkoon (let be) sinun (your) nimesi (name);

tulkoon (let come) sinun (your) valtakuntasi (kingdom);

tapahtukoon (let happen) sinun (your) tahtosi (will),

niin kuin (just as) taivaassa (in heaven),

niin myös (so also) maan päällä (on earth).

Anna (give) meille (to us) tänä päivänä (this day) meidän (our) jokapäiväinen (daily) leipämme (bread);

ja (and) anna (give) meille (to us) meidän (our) velkamme (debts) anteeksi (forgiveness),

niin kuin (just as) mekin (we also) annamme (give) anteeksi (forgiveness) velallisillemme (to our debtors);

äläkä (and do not) saata (lead) meitä (us) kiusaukseen (into temptation),

vaan (but) päästä (deliver) meidät (us) pahasta (from evil).

Aamen (Amen).

Phonetic Pronunciation

Isä meidän (EE-sah MAY-dahn)

Isä (EE-sah) meidän (MAY-dahn),

joka (YOH-kah) olet (OH-let) taivaissa (TIE-vai-sah),

pyhitetty (PYH-hi-teht-ty) olkoon (OHL-kohn) sinun (SEE-noon) nimesi (NEE-meh-see);

tulkoon (TOOL-kohn) sinun (SEE-noon) valtakuntasi (VAHL-tah-koon-tah-see);

tapahtukoon (TAH-pah-too-kohn) sinun (SEE-noon) tahtosi (TAH-ho-see),

niin kuin (NEEN koo-een) taivaassa (TIE-vah-sah),

niin myös (NEEN myuhs) maan (MAHN) päällä (PAEH-lah).

Anna (AHN-nah) meille (MAY-leh) tänä (TAH-nah) päivänä (PAI-vah-nah) meidän (MAY-dahn) jokapäiväinen (YOH-kah-pai-vai-nehn) leipämme (LAY-pahm-meh);

ja (yah) anna (AHN-nah) meille (MAY-leh) meidän (MAY-dahn) velkamme (VEL-kahm-meh) anteeksi (AHN-tehk-see),

niin kuin (NEEN koo-een) mekin (MEH-kin) annamme (AHN-nah-meh) anteeksi (AHN-tehk-see) velallisillemme (VEH-lahl-lee-sil-lehm-meh);

äläkä (AH-lah-kah) saata (SAH-tah) meitä (MAY-tah) kiusaukseen (KEE-oo-sah-ook-sehn),

vaan (VAHN) päästä (PAEH-stah) meidät (MAY-daht) pahasta (PAH-hah-stah).

Aamen (AH-men).

Understanding the Finnish Alphabet

Alphabet

- Finnish uses the **Latin alphabet** with **29 letters**: **A, B, C, D, E, F, G, H, I, J, K, L, M, N, O, P, Q, R, S, Š, T, U, V, W, X, Y, Z, Ž, Ä, Ö**.
- Letters **Q, W, X, Z** appear mostly in foreign words, names, or loanwords.
- Letters **Š, Ž** are used only in loanwords and foreign names.
- Each letter generally corresponds to a **distinct sound**, making Finnish highly phonetic.

Letter Sounds Differ from English

- **A** = *ah* (talo ≈ tah-lo).
- **E** = *eh* (vesi ≈ veh-si).
- **I** = *ee* (kiwi ≈ kee-vee).
- **O** = *oh* (koti ≈ koh-ti).
- **U** = *oo* (kupu ≈ koo-poo).
- **Y** = fronted *ü*, like German ü (tyttö ≈ tü-t-tö).
- **Ä** = *a* as in cat (pää ≈ pah).
- **Ö** = like French *peur* or German ö (söpö ≈ sö-pö).
- **J** = *y* as in yes (juna ≈ yoo-na).
- **K / P / T / L / M / N / R / S / V / H** = pronounced roughly as in English.
- **G** = used mainly in loanwords; pronounced hard *g* (golf ≈ golf).
- **Double vowels** = held longer (talo = tah-lo vs. taalo = tah-loo).
- **Double consonants** = held longer (mato ≈ ma-to vs. matto ≈ mat-to).
- **R** = trilled or tapped.

Accent Marks

- Finnish **does not use accent marks** in standard orthography.
- Stress is **fixed on the first syllable** of the word.
- Loanwords may retain accents from other languages.

Understanding Finnish Grammar

Nouns and Gender
- Finnish **has no grammatical gender**; the same words are used for "he" and "she."
- Nouns are **inflected for 15 cases** (e.g., nominative, genitive, partitive, inessive, elative, illative, adessive, ablative, allative, essive, translative, instructive, abessive, comitative, prolative).
- Plural forms vary by case:
  - *talo* → *talot* (house → houses, nominative plural).
  - *taloa* → *taloja* (house → houses, partitive plural).

Articles
- Finnish **does not use definite or indefinite articles**; context determines definiteness.

Adjectives
- Agree with nouns in **number and case**:
  - *iso talo* = big house.
  - *isot talot* = big houses.
- Usually placed **before the noun**.

Pronouns
- Subject: *minä, sinä, hän, me, te, he.*
- Object: same forms, case-marked (*minua, sinua, häntä, meitä, teitä, heitä*).
- Possessive suffixes often replace possessive pronouns: *taloni* = my house.
- Reflexive: *itse.*
- Finnish is **not pro-drop**, but subject pronouns are often omitted because verb endings indicate person.

Verbs
- Conjugate for **person, number, tense, mood, and voice**.
- Key tenses:
  - **Present tense**: *minä puhun* (I speak).
  - **Past tense (imperfect)**: *minä puhuin* (I spoke).
  - **Perfect tense**: *minä olen puhunut* (I have spoken).
  - **Pluperfect tense**: *minä olin puhunut* (I had spoken).

- Moods: indicative, conditional (*puhuisin* = I would speak), imperative, potential (*puhunen* = I might speak).
- Verb infinitives: main, first, second, third forms.

Word Order

- Standard **SVO** (subject-verb-object): *Minä luen kirjaa* (I read a book).
- Flexible due to extensive case marking; word order often emphasizes topic or focus.

Questions and Negation

- Yes/No questions use intonation: *Puhutko suomea?* (Do you speak Finnish?).
- Question words: *kuka* (who), *mitä* (what), *missä* (where), *milloin* (when), *miksi* (why), *miten* (how).
- Negation uses a special verb *ei* that agrees with the subject:
  - *Minä en puhu* = I do not speak.
  - *Sinä et puhu* = You do not speak.

Prepositions

- Finnish uses **postpositions and case endings** instead of prepositions:
  - *talossa* = in the house (inessive).
  - *talosta* = from the house (elative).
  - *taloon* = into the house (illative).

Special Features

- No grammatical gender.
- Case system is central: conveys what English prepositions do.
- Word endings indicate possession, number, and grammatical relationships.
- Negation is expressed with a negative verb, not by a particle.

Chapter XXIX

Estonian

The Lords Prayer in *Eesti* (Estonian)

Meie Isa

Meie Isa,
kes Sa oled taevas,
pühitsetud olgu Su nimi;
tulgu Su kuningriik;
saagu Su tahtmine,
nagu taevas, nõnda ka maa peal.
Anna meile täna meie igapäevane leib;
ja anna meile andeks meie võlad,
nagu meiegi anname andeks oma võlglastele;
ja ära saaita meid kiusatusse,
vaid päästa meid ära kurjast.
Aamen.

Word-to-Word Translation

Meie Isa (The Our Father)

Meie (Our) **Isa,** (Father,)

kes (who) **sa** (you) **oled** (are) **taevas,** (in heaven,)

pühitsetud (sanctified) **olgu** (let be) **Su** (your) **nimi;** (name;)

tulgu (let come) **Su** (your) **kuningriik;** (kingdom;)

saagu (let be) **Su** (your) **tahtmine,** (will,)

nagu (as) **taevas,** (heaven,)

nõnda (so) **ka** (also) **maa peal.** (on earth.)

Anna (Give) **meile** (to us) **täna** (today),

meie (our) **igapäevane** (daily) **leib;** (bread;)

ja (and) **anna** (give) **meile** (to us) **andeks** (forgiveness) **meie** (our) **võlad,** (debts,)

nagu (as) **meiegi** (we also) **anname** (give) **andeks** (forgiveness) **oma** (our) **võlglastele;** (debtors;)

ja (and) **ära** (not) **lase** (lead) **meid** (us) **kiusatusse,** (into temptation,)

vaid (but) **päästa** (deliver) **meid** (us) **ära** (from) **kurjast.** (evil.)

Aamen. (Amen.)

Phonetic Pronunciation

Meie Isa (MEH-yeh EE-sah)

Meie (MEH-yeh) **Isa,** (EE-sah),

kes (kehs) **sa** (sah) **oled** (OH-led) **taevas,** (TIE-vahs),

pühitsetud (PYH-heet-seh-tood) **olgu** (OHL-goo) **sinu** (SEE-noo)
nimi; (NEE-mee);

sinu (SEE-noo) **riik** (REEK) **tulgu;** (TOOL-goo);

sinu (SEE-noo) **tahe** (TAH-heh) **sündigu,** (SÜN-dee-goo),

nõnda (NUN-dah) **nagu** (NAH-goo) **taevas,** (TIE-vahs),

nõnda (NUN-dah) **ka** (kah) **maa** (MAH) **peal.** (peh-AHL).

Anna (AHN-nah) **meile** (MEI-leh) **täna** (TEH-nah);

meie (MEI-eh) **igapäevast** (EE-gah-pai-vahst) **leib** (LEIB);

ja (yah) **anna** (AHN-nah) **meile** (MAY-leh) **andeks** (AHN-dehks)
meie (MEH-yeh) **võlad,** (VUH-lahd),

nagu (NAH-goo) **meiegi** (MEH-yeh-gee) **andestame** (AHN-dehs-
tah-meh) **oma** (OH-mah) **võlglastele;** (VUH-lglahs-teh-leh);

ja (yah) **ära** (AH-rah) **lase** (LAH-seh) **meid** (MAY-d) **kiusatusse,**
(KEE-oo-sah-toos-seh),

vaid (vah-eed) **päästa** (PAEH-stah) **meid** (MAY-d) **ära** (EH-rah)
kurjast. (KOO-ryahst).

Aamen. (AH-men).

171

Understanding the Estonian Alphabet

Alphabet

- Estonian uses the **Latin alphabet** with **27 letters**: **A, B, D, E, F, G, H, I, J, K, L, M, N, O, P, R, S, Š, Z, Ž, T, U, V, Õ, Ä, Ö, Ü**.
- Letters **C, Q, W, X, Y** appear only in foreign words, names, or loanwords.
- Each letter generally corresponds to a **distinct sound**, making Estonian highly phonetic.

Letter Sounds Differ from English

- **A / Ä / O / Õ / U / Ö / Ü** = pure vowels, pronounced as written:
  - **A** = *ah* (maja ≈ mah-ya).
  - **Ä** = *a* as in cat (pärn ≈ pah-ern).
  - **O** = *oh* (kodu ≈ koh-doo).
  - **Õ** = unique Estonian vowel, between *uh* and *o* (õlu ≈ uh-lu).
  - **U** = *oo* (kuu ≈ koo).
  - **Ö** = like German ö or French *peur* (sööma ≈ søh-ma).
  - **Ü** = like German ü (lühi ≈ lyu-hi).
- **B / D / G** = pronounced as in English; may appear in loanwords.
- **C / F / H / J / K / L / M / N / P / R / S / Š / Z / Ž / T / V** = pronounced roughly as in English.
  - **Š** = *sh* (šokolaad ≈ shok-o-laad).
  - **Ž** = *zh* as in *measure* (žanr ≈ zhanr).
- **J** = *y* as in yes (ja ≈ yah).
- **Double vowels and consonants** = pronounced longer, which can change word meaning:
  - **sada** (hundred) vs. **saada** (to get).
  - **tuli** (fire) vs. **tulli** (customs).
- **R** = trilled or tapped.

Accent Marks

- Estonian **does not use accent marks** in native words.
- Stress is **always on the first syllable** of the word.
- Loanwords may retain accents from other languages.

Understanding Estonian Grammar

Nouns and Gender
- Estonian **has no grammatical gender**; the same words are used for "he" and "she."
- Nouns are **inflected for 14 cases** (e.g., nominative, genitive, partitive, illative, inessive, elative, allative, adessive, ablative, translative, terminative, essive, abessive, comitative).
- Plural forms depend on the case:
  - *maja* → *majad* (house → houses, nominative plural).
  - *maja* → *maju* (partitive singular/plural, depending on context).

Articles
- Estonian **does not use definite or indefinite articles**; context indicates definiteness.

Adjectives
- Agree with nouns in **number and case**:
  - *suur maja* = big house.
  - *suured majad* = big houses.
- Usually placed **before the noun**.

Pronouns
- Subject: *mina, sina, tema, meie, teie, nemad.*
- Object: case-marked forms (*mind, sind, teda, meid, teid, neid*).
- Possessive: expressed using possessive suffixes or *minu, sinu, tema, meie, teie, nende.*
- Reflexive: *ise.*
- Estonian is **not pro-drop**, but subject pronouns can be omitted when verb endings make the subject clear.

Verbs
- Conjugate for **person, number, tense, mood, and voice**.
- Key tenses:
  - **Present tense**: *ma räägin* (I speak).
  - **Past tense**: *ma rääkisin* (I spoke).
  - **Perfect tense**: *ma olen rääkinud* (I have spoken).
- Moods: indicative, conditional (*rääkiksin* = I would speak), imperative, potential (*rääkine* = I might speak).

- Verb forms include **infinitives and participles**.

Word Order
- Standard **SVO** (subject-verb-object): *Ma loen raamatut* (I read a book).
- Flexible due to rich case system; word order often highlights focus or contrast.

Questions and Negation
- Yes/No questions use intonation: *Kas sa räägid eesti keelt?* (You speak Estonian language?).
- Question words: *kes* (who), *mis* (what), *kus* (where), *millal* (when), *miks* (why), *kuidas* (how).
- Negation uses a negative verb *ei*, which agrees with the subject:
  - *Ma ei räägi* = I do not speak.
  - *Sa ei räägi* = You do not speak.

Prepositions
- Estonian relies mainly on **case endings** rather than prepositions:
  - *majas* = in the house (inessive).
  - *majast* = from the house (elative).
  - *majja* = into the house (illative).

Special Features
- No grammatical gender.
- Extensive case system conveys relationships normally expressed with prepositions.
- Possession can be indicated via suffixes or possessive pronouns.
- Negation is expressed with a separate negative verb, not a particle.

Chapter XXX

Hungarian

The Lords Prayer in *Magyar* (Hungarian)

Miatyánk

Miatyánk,
aki vagy a mennyekben,
szenteltessék meg a te neved;
jöjjön el a te országod;
legyen meg a te akaratod,
amint a mennyben, úgy a földön is.
Mindennapi kenyerünket add meg nekünk ma;
és bocsásd meg vétkeinket,
miképpen mi is megbocsátunk az ellenfeleinknek;
és ne vígy minket kísértésbe,
de szabadíts meg a gonosztól.
Ámen.

Word-to-Word Translation

Miatyánk (The Our Father)

Miatyánk, (Our Father,)

aki (who) **vagy** (are) **a** (the) **mennyekben,** (in heavens,)

szenteltessék (be sanctified) **meg** (completeness particle) **a** (the) **te** (your) **neved;** (name;)

jöjjön (come) **el** (forth) **a** (the) **te** (your) **országod;** (kingdom;)

legyen (let be) **meg** (complete) **a** (the) **te** (your) **akaratod,** (will,)

amint (as) **a** (the) **mennyben,** (in heaven,) **úgy** (so) **a** (the) **földön** (on earth) **is.** (also.)

Mindennapi (daily) **kenyerünket** (our bread) **add** (give) **meg** (completeness particle) **nekünk** (to us) **ma;** (today;)

és (and) **bocsásd** (forgive) **meg** (completeness particle) **vétkeinket,** (our sins/debts,)

miképpen (just as) **mi** (we) **is** (also) **megbocsátunk** (forgive) **az** (the) **ellenfeleinknek;** (our enemies;)

és (and) **ne** (not) **vígy** (lead) **minket** (us) **kísértésbe,** (into temptation,)

de (but) **szabadíts** (deliver) **meg** (completeness particle) **a** (the) **gonosztól.** (evil-from.)

Ámen. (Amen.)

Phonetic Pronunciation

Miatyánk (MEE-ah-tyahnk)

Miatyánk (MEE-ah-tyahnk),

aki (AH-kee) **vagy** (vahd) **a** (ah) **mennyekben** (MEHN-yehk-ben),

szenteltessék (SEN-tel-teh-shehk) **meg** (meg) **a** (ah) **te** (teh) **neved**
(NEH-ved);

jöjjön (YOO-yohn) **el** (el) **a** (ah) **te** (teh) **országod** (OHR-shah-god);

legyen (LEH-dyen) **meg** (meg) **a** (ah) **te** (teh) **akaratod** (AH-kah-
rah-tod),

amint (AH-mint) **a** (ah) **mennyben,** (MEHN-ben) **úgy** (OO-gy) **a**
(ah) **földön** (FURL-durn) **is** (ees),

Mindennapi (MEEN-den-nah-pee) **kenyerünket** (KEH-nyer-oon-
ket) **add** (odd) **meg** (meg) **nekünk** (NEH-kunk) **ma** (mah);

és (aysh) **bocsásd** (BOH-chahshd) **meg** (meg) **vétkeinket** (VEHT-
kayn-ket),

miképpen (MEE-kay-ppen) **mi** (mee) **is** (ees) **megbocsátunk**
(MEG-boh-chah-toonk) **az** (ahz) **ellenfeleinknek** (EL-len-feh-leink-
nek);

és (aysh) **ne** (neh) **vígy** (VEE-dy) **minket** (MINK-et) **kísértésbe**
(KEE-shehr-taysh-beh),

de (deh) **szabadíts** (SAA-bah-deets) **meg** (meg) **a** (ah) **gonosztól**
(GOH-nos-tol);

Ámen (AH-men).

Understanding the Hungarian Alphabet

Alphabet
- Hungarian uses the **Latin alphabet** with **44 letters**, including digraphs and diacritics:
  A, Á, B, C, Cs, D, Dz, Dzs, E, É, F, G, Gy, H, I, Í, J, K, L, Ly, M, N, Ny, O, Ó, Ö, Ő, P, Q, R, S, Sz, T, Ty, U, Ú, Ü, Ű, V, W, X, Y, Z, Zs.
- Letters **Q, W, X, Y** appear mainly in foreign words or names.
- Digraphs (Cs, Dz, Dzs, Gy, Ly, Ny, Sz, Ty, Zs) are **treated as single letters** in alphabetization.

Letter Sounds Differ from English
- **A / Á** = short *ah* and long *aah* (ház ≈ haahz).
- **E / É** = short *eh* and long *ay* (szék ≈ saayk).
- **I / Í** = short *ih* and long *ee* (kis ≈ kish, írás ≈ ee-raash).
- **O / Ó / Ö / Ő** = short, long, and front rounded vowels (ló ≈ loh, öröm ≈ ö-röm, ősz ≈ ő-sz).
- **U / Ú / Ü / Ű** = short, long, front rounded (tűz ≈ t-üüz, fű ≈ f-üü).
- **C** = *ts* (cica ≈ tsi-tsa).
- **Cs** = *ch* as in church (család ≈ cha-laad).
- **Dz / Dzs** = *ds* and *j* sounds (dzsem ≈ d-jem).
- **G / Gy** = hard *g* vs. palatalized *dy* (gyerek ≈ dy-e-rek).
- **H / J / K / L / Ly / M / N / Ny / P / R / S / Sz / T / Ty / V / Z / Zs** = pronounced with Hungarian rules:
  - **Ly** = palatalized *l* (hajlít ≈ hay-lit).
  - **Sz** = *s* as in see (szép ≈ sayp).
  - **S** = *sh* (sok ≈ shok).
  - **Zs** = *zh* as in measure (zsemle ≈ zhem-le).
- **R** = trilled.
- **Double vowels and consonants** = usually indicate length:
  - **két** (two) vs. **kettő** (the number two).
  - **nn / ll / ss** lengthened slightly.

Accent Marks
- **Acute accents** indicate vowel length (á, é, í, ó, ú, ő, ű).
- Stress is **always on the first syllable**.
- Loanwords may retain accents from other languages.

Understanding Hungarian Grammar

Nouns and Gender
- Hungarian **has no grammatical gender**; the same words are used for "he" and "she."
- Nouns are **inflected for number and case**, with **18 grammatical cases** including nominative, accusative, dative, instrumental, inessive, superessive, adessive, ablative, allative, elative, illative, translative, terminative, essive-formal, causal-final, temporal, distributive, and sociative.
- Plural: usually formed with **-k** (*ház* → *házak* = house → houses).

Articles
- Definite: *a, az* = the (before consonant / vowel).
- Indefinite: *egy* = a, an.
- Articles agree in number, not gender.

Adjectives
- Agree with nouns in **number** and **definiteness**:
  - *nagy ház* = big house.
  - *nagy házak* = big houses.
- Usually placed **before the noun.**

Pronouns
- Subject: *én, te, ő, mi, ti, ők.*
- Object: *engem, téged, őt, minket, titeket, őket.*
- Possessive: suffixes attached to nouns (*házam* = my house).
- Reflexive: *magam, magad, maga, magunk, magatok, maguk.*
- Hungarian is **not pro-drop**, but subject pronouns are often omitted because verb conjugation indicates person.

Verbs
- Conjugated for **person, number, tense, mood, definiteness, and sometimes polarity.**
- Two conjugation patterns: definite vs. indefinite objects.
- Key tenses:
  - **Present tense**: *beszélek* (I speak).
  - **Past tense**: *beszéltem* (I spoke).
  - **Future tense**: usually formed with *fog* + *infinitive* (*fogok beszélni* = I will speak).

- Moods: indicative, conditional (*beszélnék* = I would speak), imperative.

Word Order
- Standard **SVO** (subject-verb-object): Flexible due to emphasis and focus.
- Topic–focus structure is important; elements in focus usually appear immediately before the verb.

Questions and Negation
- Yes/No questions use intonation: *Beszélsz magyarul?* (You speak Hungarian?).
- Question words: *ki* (who), *mi* (what), *hol* (where), *mikor* (when), *miért* (why), *hogyan* (how).
- Negation: *nem* before the verb (*Nem beszélek* = I do not speak).
- Double negatives are common and required with negative pronouns (*Senki sem jött* = Nobody came).

Prepositions / Postpositions
- Hungarian uses both **prepositions and postpositions**, but case endings often replace them:
  - *házban* = in the house (inessive).
  - *házból* = from the house (elative).
  - *házhoz* = to the house (allative).

Special Features
- No grammatical gender.
- Verb conjugation distinguishes **definite vs. indefinite objects**.
- Cases are central to expressing spatial, temporal, and grammatical relations.
- Negation uses a separate word (*nem*) and interacts with verb forms.

www.ingramcontent.com/pod-product-compliance
Lightning Source LLC
LaVergne TN
LVHW041317080426
835513LV00008B/499